A CAPABLE JOURNALIST

Dedicated to all those 'contacts'
who are essential to any reporter's work

A CAPABLE JOURNALIST

DEREK BELLIS

First impression: 2019

Cover photograph: Sion Jones
Cover design: Y Lolfa

ISBN: 978 1 78461 725 7

Published and printed in Wales
on paper from well-maintained forests by
Y Lolfa Cyf., Talybont, Ceredigion SY24 5HE
website www.ylolfa.com
e-mail ylolfa@ylolfa.com
tel 01970 832 304
fax 832 782

Praise for the author

Derek Bellis is one of the country's most respected journalists and epitomises the values of our great profession. To enjoy and sustain a career which has spanned seven decades is a remarkable achievement and stands as testament to Derek's brilliant ability. Trustworthy, tenacious and utterly devoted to reporting the truth, Derek is a true legend of the industry.

Dominic Herbert
News Editor, *Daily Mirror*

'75, and still getting the headlines' ... '80, a journalist to be respected' ... '86, and still writing!' Derek represents a style of journalism that commands our admiration. At a time of massive changes in the world of journalism, Derek has more than survived.

As a youngster living in Conwy, I spent a great deal of time on the quay enchanted by the activities at R.E. Jones' printing works – putting a newspaper to bed in a manner that now belongs to the past. The digital age has taken over. But it is not only the technique of producing the paper that has changed but the very journalism itself, and Derek Bellis has more than withstood the changes and is as respected today as he was when he started his career on the old *North Wales Pioneer* and progressed to national dailies – the greatly missed *News Chronicle* and *Daily Herald*.

A man of his own 'square mile', born in Colwyn Bay and still living amongst friends and acquaintances with whom he has shared so many experiences. If ever a journalist knew his people and their background, that man is Derek Bellis. Our families would meet often at the swimming pool and then at election times at rallies and counts. Derek was always fair as he reported various events. As we turn the pages of his memoir, we shall have a glimpse of the life of a journalist at its very best.

Lord (Roger) Roberts of Llandudno

Foreword

OF THE MANY profound changes in a 21st-century newsroom, the most troubling is the silence of the phones. Reporters still pitch ideas for stories and features, of course, writing long or short emails in the quest to spark an editor's interest. Their proposals come in every day. But the tales that freelance journalists offer tend to have a specialist slant, and an entire class of reporters has all but vanished.

In 2019, one regular freelance might offer arts stories while another picks up scoops in defence. A third specialises in finding housing stories while a fourth covers the NHS, supplementing, corroborating and competing with the staff journalists who cover the same beat.

What's gone missing is people like Derek Bellis.

For more than 50 years, Derek has run a news agency covering north Wales. He and others like him were once the lifeblood of national news. On news desks in Manchester and London, the phones rang with quirky or disturbing tales from courts, councils and other local sources. These journalists raised families by using their wits to turn local events into national column centimetres, often paid at rates such as 20p per published line (it was called lineage). Selling their stories to news editors and then dictating it immediately to a bank of copytakers over a landline telephone, these stringers, as they were known, were part of the fabric of the fourth estate, holding local power to account by knowing how to focus national attention on injustice, and entertaining the nation with local eccentricities.

After spells as a tram conductor and as a strawberry picker in the Conwy Valley, getting up at 6 a.m. to cycle eight miles to a farm at Eglwysbach, Derek found his calling on the previously owned *North Wales Pioneer* – not to be confused with the present one – a weekly paper of such limited resources it could not afford to pay photographers to provide pictures. It illustrated its pages with 'blocks', or photographs of stars to be seen at local cinemas, provided free by film companies. A sombre front page report from an inquest might be illustrated with a picture of Jane Fonda, or another star of the time 'at the Arcadia next week'.

Yet the *Pioneer*, followed by the *Northants Evening Telegraph*, *Liverpool Daily Post and Echo*, the *News Chronicle* and the *Daily Herald*, and weekend shifts on the *News of the World* in Manchester, taught Derek our trade, and at 86 he is still at it, sending story ideas and tips for investigations to national news desks.

In Britain, national titles have embraced the digital future and are starting to thrive again. In less than a decade we have gone from awe at the pace of change to a degree of excitement at what the new world offers us as storytellers. But the damage done to the local reporting infrastructure in that decade, and the loss of entrepreneurs such as Derek, is a matter of great regret.

He is an exception: he survived. His book, with its strong sense of place, recalls a time when chapel was a dominant feature of life (usually three times every Sunday, and in Welsh, which was not taught in primary school). It is published in a world that has been transformed. Derek has chronicled the transition from one era to the other, and I am proud to count him as a contributor to the *Sunday Times*.

Tim Rayment
Deputy News Editor, *The Sunday Times*

Preface

JOURNALISM HAS GIVEN me more than 60 years of enjoyment and fulfilment. I am grateful for rich experiences which won't be surpassed by my successors because modern journalism has changed dramatically, unfortunately not for the better. Now the craft is often governed by cold-eyed accountants and monopolies whose consuming interest is in the bottom line and the number of 'clicks' that stories receive online.

Sadly many of the family-run newspapers, which for generations served communities and trained young journalists, have disappeared. Staffs have been cut to such an extent that it is no longer possible to provide the comprehensive coverage on which local weeklies and dailies should depend.

Owners claim that 'multi-media' is now the solution, with journalists being invited to reapply for their own jobs or face redundancy. They're expected to operate a video camera and make films, sometimes like asking a trapeze artist to double up as a lion tamer. Yet recent research has shown that while newspapers can be read for an average of 40 minutes a day, online visitors spend as little as 30 seconds there.

When I started in 1950 news was king. The scoop was obtained by hard graft and great contacts.

I worked on thriving evening newspapers. And in Manchester, one of the biggest news centres in the world, national papers employed huge staffs of reporters and sub-editors. When there was a disaster at Manchester Airport the *Express* exported its northern sub-editors' desk to a nearby hotel to plan the words and the pages.

Now the *Express* doesn't have a single staff reporter in the north of England and its famous office in Great Ancoats Street, the Black Lubianka as it was once called, is no more. The *Daily Mirror* has a handful of reporters manning its northern operation.

My book is about fun and tragedy, achievement and disaster. For more than half a century I've run a news agency covering north Wales. I started my career on the *North Wales Pioneer*, a weekly paper in Colwyn Bay. Later I was with the *Northants Evening Telegraph, Liverpool Daily Post and Echo*, the late lamented *News Chronicle* and the *Daily Herald*, with many years' weekend experience on the *News of the World* in Manchester. I've also contributed scores of voice reports for Radio Wales.

Records have been kept of nearly every story, most of them pre-computer in large exercise books which have now become musty. Among my stories are the Investiture of Prince Charles (for the *Daily Express*); the inquest where the Jeremy Thorpe-Norman Scott sensation originated; an interview for ITN with the Beatles after the death of their manager (which is still being replayed worldwide); a year's coverage of the north Wales child abuse tribunal; the loss of 15 holidaymakers in a river tragedy; the astonishing story of a chapel minister who mutilated and photographed dead bodies; murders which have shocked the nation; stories of Welsh saboteurs and firebombers; and scores of humorous and zany tales. And I've met or been in the same room as 11 prime ministers!

At 86 I'm still at it, part-time, partly because of my love of writing news and features, and because I was misled into taking a pension with Equitable Life – the biggest financial disaster of my life. I hope I retain the instinct for a good story that I possessed as a cub reporter in those early years.

Like my contemporaries I had to take two years away from the job when National Service beckoned. That time, in the Royal Marines, turned out to be a bonus.

The book title, *A Capable Journalist*, is how I was described, maybe reluctantly, during an animated debate at the old North Wales Police Authority when stories of mine in two national papers, which were perfectly accurate, were criticised. At the time the chief constable was Richard Brunstrom, famous for his anti-speeding campaigns – and those cameras. He was the most controversial and interesting police chief in Britain and a rich source for stories.

I have written this book as honestly as I can, intending no offence, giving what I hope is an accurate recollection of more than 60 years in a business in which no two days were the same.

Thanks to family and friends for assisting my memory.

And thanks too to Eirian Jones, English-language editor at Y Lolfa, for her expertise and patience. She's the most skilful and erudite sub-editor I've ever encountered!

Also thanks to John Lawson-Reay for his great photographic reminders of the past.

A few years ago I was presented with a Lifetime Achievement Award by the National Association of Press Agencies. More recently I had my greatest honour when, at an event in Cardiff fronted by newscaster Huw Edwards, I received the Outstanding Contribution Award at the Welsh Media Awards, organised by the Journalists' Charity. I just hope those awards reflect my journalism – not my longevity!

Derek Bellis
September 2019

Contents

1   Those halcyon days   15

2   How it all began   19

3   Such an enjoyable life   24

4   Serving the Queen – by order!   29

5   Heat and sand   34

6   North Wales – Northants – Merseyside   39

7   Life in the 'Fleet Street of the north'   48

8   From Manchester back to my roots   55

9   My own boss   60

10   All the news fit to print   67

11   Amazing inquests   72

12   The Investiture   79

13   Some violent campaigns   90

14   Saturday night fever   95

15   A date with the Beatles   99

16   Crime and punishment   104

17   Great characters   114

18   A strange tragedy in the hills   121

19   Sea rescues   123

20   The quirky and unusual   128

21 The biggest fire I ever saw 137

22 Politics is fun 140

23 Among those I have met 149

24 Truly greats 153

25 Those with smiling faces 158

26 Famous funerals 160

27 A little night music – and police generosity 163

28 Law and order 165

29 A very personal mystery 169

30 Thursday's man 170

31 Prayers for a hospice 172

32 The day the sea invaded Towyn 174

33 Don't always believe them 176

34 What an uplifting story 179

35 The greatest comedian ever 182

36 'The road to opportunity' 184

37 Political correctness 186

38 Lost in care 189

39 Fake news? 195

Epilogue 197

1

Those halcyon days

THE TWO ELEMENTS of journalism that appeal to me most are the enjoyment – and exposing what is wrong by shining a light where it's unwelcome.

When in 1950 I climbed the stairs above Lloyds Bank in Colwyn Bay to start my career as a junior reporter in the offices of the *North Wales Pioneer* (I think the salary was 18 shillings a week, in cash every Friday), I little dreamed what a lifetime of opportunity was opening.

Some of the fun could not be better portrayed in a *Carry On* film. An example was when hundreds of Welsh protesters flew down a hillside like a crowd of dervishes to ruin the opening of the Tryweryn Dam, prodding the VIP guests with umbrellas as they tried to reach that eternal favourite for public servants and councillors – the free lunch marquee.

And I can still see the shapely blonde being brought to safety by a breeches buoy from a German coaster, beached by a storm on the sands in Penmaenmawr. It was a scene captured by national TV but the blonde remained dumb when we tried to question her in the warmth of the sailing club. 'Leave her alone, she speaks only German,' we were instructed. A local photographer retorted, 'No she doesn't, she's from Llandudno. I remember her from school.' The poor lady had been invited aboard by the ship's engineer overnight and her embarrassment was complete as cameras whirled.

Then there was the story of two drunken young Irishmen at Holyhead who missed a ferry home – so pinched a trawler hoping to sail back to Dublin. After making a desperate mayday call the trawler, *Le Bon Mawr*, was found off Wylfa. The intrepid sailors had gone 12 miles in the wrong direction.

They were brought back to Holyhead after an operation costing thousands involving the local lifeboat and an RAF helicopter. As Ray Steadman, the RNLI launching officer, put it: 'They had no experience of the sea whatever, they didn't even know how to switch on the cabin light.' The Irishmen had one piece of good luck – they were not prosecuted.

Then there was the story of a pensioner in Anglesey who tried to retrieve his wheelie-bin when it was blown out to sea and he had to be rescued in it by lifeboat.

I hope that in my career I've helped to expose a few wrongs, injustices, and even, partly, the harrowing tale of a woman wrongly sectioned and imprisoned.

In recent years I must confess to poking fun at political correctness, hypocrisy, and health and safety regulations. There's the costly nonsense of diversity training and the verbal stupidities like the title of chair – an inanimate object with four legs – to describe the chairman, chairwoman or whoever presides. It's my proud boast never to have used chair, or in my view that other abomination, Ms, in print. Sometimes, however, sub-editors (there are a few left!) insert these descriptions on my behalf.

Political correctness was in its early days in 1989 when trading standards officials took 'Eggy' Williams to court because of his nickname. Eggy, who sold 20,000 eggs each week, was given an absolute discharge by magistrates in Abergele for the crime of using Eggy Williams on his invoices instead of his full name, even though his full address and VAT number appeared. 'No one knows him other than as Eggy Williams,' said his solicitor. 'That's the name he's known by his friends, neighbours, customers and even his solicitor. It might not be his official name but that's how he's known to everyone.'

In those days political correctness was first being embraced and then expanded by chief executives, chief constables and sundry officials. In the Second World War's fight for freedom, could it have been envisaged that one day a man would have to pay hundreds of pounds to a court – for smoking a cig in the cab of his truck parked for lunch? He was 'nicked' by a council dog warden – 'civil enforcement officer' or 'accredited person' as the men in black are called. For some of them Stasi is a better name.

The owner of a Colwyn Bay fishing bait shop had to pay £900 in a fine and costs – for having undersized crabs. 'I know of two men with cocaine who were fined less,' he complained bitterly after the case. 'Fisheries officers walked into my shop and said they had the same powers as police and could arrest me and close down the business.'

It's because of such misuses of power – and these are only minor examples – that journalism still has such a role in exposing and ridiculing the lengths to which officialdom will go to impose its will.

But, when I started, Britain was recovering from a world war, with a deficit even greater than today's, and ex-servicemen and women would have little patience for town halls or ministries with a belief that their task was not to serve the people but to control them.

I have spent hundreds of days reporting from courts. I view the British judicial system as the finest in the world. It might not be perfect but it's the best we can do. I have particular admiration for magistrates who give their services free – just like councillors did in another age. Most of them are serious, conscientious and painstaking. It would be a crime were their work to be taken over entirely by professionals.

As for criminal lawyers – those who can't think on their feet in court soon lose their reputation. I once read a claim that eventually barristers become so desensitised by their daily appointment with crime that compassion is lost. With good lawyers that's not the case, just as with good journalists. And judges? Pompous, yes, some of them, and bad-tempered too. But I have seen some of the finest minds in Britain on the judicial bench. There are some, however, whose rudeness would not be countenanced in another profession. My major criticism of the system is that if there is an injustice it takes too long to put it right. Sometimes a defendant's fate can be decided by a matter of feet – a tough judge in one court, a lenient one next door.

I do not like defendants being caged in docks such as at Caernarfon, where they sit with headphones just like those Nazis did in Nuremberg.

Returning to the crusade against smoking (no cigarette has touched my lips in 50 years!). In the First World War 'Woodbine Willie' was a famous pastor who ministered to those poor troops in the trenches on the Western Front, handing out comforting 'fags' as he spoke to them. These days he'd be hauled into court by 'enforcement officers' for encouraging smoking in the workplace!

2

How it all began

I WAS TOLD that, when I was a baby, a cricket ball lofted from the school playground adjoining our home, and landed on the pillow in my pram while I was fast asleep. Maybe that was a precursor of things to come... that luck was usually on my side.

Our family home was Radcliffe House, a brick-built three-floor building which my grandparents had used to take in holidaymakers and lodgers. Among the visitors were members of the famous Gladstone family who would journey by train from their home in Hawarden, 35 miles away, then by horse-drawn carriage a few hundred yards from Colwyn Bay railway station.

My earliest memories were 'racing' the Irish mail train (steam, of course) along East Parade on my tricycle, and once as a toddler wandering into Eirias Park to watch a fire brigade demonstration, while frantic parents searched for me. Then I recall raising a stick to beat off a girl who was being unpleasant to my sister Joan in the same park.

I was born in a nursing home in Old Colwyn to my mother May, a former nurse, and father Hugh. My father spent half a century in the Post Office, starting as a teenage telegram boy and finishing as deputy head postmaster for Llandudno and Colwyn Bay. He belonged to a breed which has literally died out – those who could operate Morse code. For a time he worked at Land's End radio station, and during the Second World War served in the RAF. He was a mobile radio operator and, after D-Day, travelled through Europe before the end of the war found him in Oldenburg, Germany. He had copperplate handwriting which, unfortunately, I didn't inherit.

When I was a toddler the family stayed on a farm near Bala. This gave me two lasting memories – the farmer strangling a hen in front of us so we could eat it for dinner, and my father performing an act of bravery, putting his own life at risk, to lure a chasing bull away from his wife and two children.

It was in Radcliffe House one Sunday morning that I heard Neville Chamberlain on the radio at 11 a.m. announcing that we were at war, words that were to change all our lives. I was only six but sensed that something awful was about to happen.

Chapel was a dominant feature of life – usually three times every Sunday. With Welsh not being taught at primary school nor spoken at home, I was at a disadvantage. Those 35-minute sermons, often by dramatic and over-emotional preachers, I found difficult to understand. I complained to my mother. 'It doesn't matter, it's the atmosphere that counts,' she insisted.

Each Sunday morning children were called to deliver an 'Adnod', a verse, or perhaps several, from the Bible, learned, sometimes with feverish haste, the previous night. As a very small boy my first offering had been 'Duw Cariad Yw' (God is Love). As the years went by the verses became longer and longer, the Beatitudes in their entirety. But if a sudden crisis arose, 'Duw Cariad Yw' was always in reserve.

Sometimes I would be hauled off to midweek preaching meetings to chapels filled to capacity. Soon Salem was deprived of many of its menfolk – my own father included – as they were called up for the war. They would return on leave in their uniforms, to be feted as heroes. Little did I imagine that a few years hence I too would also return in uniform. Remarkably, all the men survived the Second World War unharmed.

Chapel-going is now relegated to the past. My theory is that in Wales chapel attendance switched half a century ago to worship of another kind – of the language.

We left Radcliffe House, bought by the nearby Wireless College which trained hundreds of Merchant Navy radio officers. The house was turned into a lecture theatre. I didn't step inside again until 40 years later when it had another role. I was there to cover an industrial tribunal.

I went to Conway Road council school, ruled with a rod of iron by a headmaster called Griffiths. There was also a devoted senior teacher called Miss Allen from whom we learned more than in any year of our lives. In Form 5 we watched through the window as hundreds of tanks passed by, en route (we assumed) for Liverpool docks to be ready for D-Day.

Unlike modern-day facilities, the school toilet was in the yard, so if it was raining you got wet. The boys were beside a wall six feet high, the girls immediately on the other side. Disgustingly, the lads would aim high... but then boys will be boys! I was thinking about this when I heard that the Children's Commissioner for Wales was complaining about the standard of school toilets.

My best pal was Peter Gresley Jones, to whose home I was instructed to flee from school should there be an air raid. After a distinguished banking career he's now back home in north Wales and our friendship has resumed.

For a young boy, wartime was often an adventure. From the top of Bryn Euryn, the local hillside where we played our own war games, we spotted high in the sky a German aircraft, probably a spotter plane. Below us swooped a solitary Spitfire and hopefully we pointed skywards to the pilot, indicating where we had seen the Luftwaffe!

Sometimes we could watch sea convoys heading towards the Mersey – merchant ships, destroyers, even aircraft carriers, and some damaged vessels limping behind.

The Royal Artillery, based a few miles away in Kinmel Camp, fired blanks from their 25-pounders on the sands. (Sixty years later, in the bush of Western Australia on holiday with my wife Shirley, I met an Australian ex-gunner who'd met his wife on a night off in Rhyl while based at Kinmel. Small world!)

Sometimes we heard real explosions too, with sea mines being washed ashore after storms.

The loudest noise I've ever heard was one Christmas when a landmine landed by parachute in the village of Llanddulas, five miles away. It was an event which was to end for all time a dispute about whether a duck pond should remain!

The war, for all its lighter moments for adventure-seeking schoolboys, nevertheless dominated the lives of everyone, and particularly our parents.

In December 1941, just before Christmas, I heard the radio news in the afternoon announcing the sinking of the warships *Prince of Wales* and *Repulse* by the Japanese, off Malaya. Hundreds of sailors drowned that terrible day. In those times counselling of families was unknown. The bereaved had to rely on relatives and friends, churches or chapels, grit their teeth and get on with their war. A neighbour's son, part of a bomber crew, was killed. It seemed a tragic inevitability. Each Remembrance Sunday I think about Wilfred, who is buried locally.

Most days, until later in the war, I cycled to school with a gas mask around my neck in its package. On the eve of my 11th birthday I was one of 36 chosen candidates who took the 11-plus examination to obtain a place at Colwyn Bay County School (later to become a grammar school, subsequently a comprehensive attended by my children and grandchildren).

It was only in later life that I appreciated the cruelty and futility of that exam. Of those 36, a single boy failed and went to the Central School instead. For him, failure could have been an experience which ruined his life. Luckily it didn't.

After the strictness of the primary school, the county school was a place of fun and very little endeavour. Girls, tennis, football and cricket filled my life. I did so badly that on one occasion I intercepted the postman to grab my summer

22

report before my mother could see it. I made amendments in an amateurish way. My mother said she was unhappy with such an untidy report and would see the headmaster as soon as term resumed. I sweated it out for several weeks, but she never made that visit. She must have realised all along what had happened, but her 'punishment' of keeping me in suspense certainly worked. I never tried it again.

It wasn't until the fifth form, with the Central Welsh Board School Certificate looming, that my mind was concentrated and school work began in earnest.

At 17 I was already working in my first job when the results came, just about achieving what in those days was a modest 'London Matriculation'. But at least there was a 'distinction' in English. This was due to an inspired teacher called John Buckland, who on a blazing Saturday afternoon took his class up the Great Orme in Llandudno to revise *The Merchant of Venice* to such an extent that I can still recall the verses he rammed into our brains, particularly 'The quality of mercy is not strained...'

There was a woman teacher whom boys would wind up cruelly and unmercifully, to the point of tears. She punished us collectively with a rebuke I can still remember, with some guilt. We were made to write a hundred times: 'There are four things that will not come back – the spoken word, the sped arrow, the past life, and the neglected opportunity.' How right she was.

3

Such an enjoyable life

THERE'S AN OLD song about youth being wasted on the young. For two years, in my first job, life was perfect.

That first summer I'd held, briefly, a job as a conductor on the trams which ran between Llandudno and Colwyn Bay and also as a strawberry picker in the Conwy Valley, getting up at 6 a.m. to cycle eight miles to the farm at Eglwysbach.

It was on a day off that a friend John Williams said to me casually: 'There's a job going on the *Pioneer*. It would suit you.' Avril Roberts, a cub reporter on the *Pioneer*, a weekly paper based in Colwyn Bay and Llandudno, was leaving – and there was a vacancy.

I presented myself at the office and was met by the senior reporter, the redoubtable Norman Tucker, also a novelist and historian. He asked me to prepare an essay on 'Why I want to be a journalist'. I couldn't type, so wrote in pen and ink.

Within a week I was on the staff. It was Norman Tucker who once told me, 'There are two kinds of people in the world: those who want their names in the paper and those who want them kept out.' He was right. Within days I had learned that it was St John Ambulance – not the incorrect St John's as one hears so often on radio and TV! – and all right, not alright; Marks and Spencer, not Spencer's. Many other dos and don'ts of style and grammar were learned which have remained with me to this day. I get irritated when I hear highly-paid national TV reporters say someone 'was sat' (instead of sitting) in their car, or, worst of all 'for free' instead of 'for nothing' or 'without payment'.

There were two weekly papers locally, the highly successful family-run *Weekly News*, and the struggling *Pioneer*.

The *Pioneer* (part of the Chronicle group whose headquarters was in Bangor) was so hard up that it couldn't afford to pay photographers to provide pictures apart from on very rare occasions. Instead, it would illustrate the paper with free 'blocks' provided by film companies – pictures of stars to be seen at local cinemas. A front page dominated by a council row or an inquest might be illustrated with a picture of Jane Fonda, Glynis Johns, Patricia Roc, the well endowed Jane Russell or some other curvaceous starlet 'at the Arcadia next week'.

Norman came in three days a week and left most of the work to me to fill the paper with news. Few activities or events went unreported. Unlike today, the cover was comprehensive.

Norman, an outstanding local historian who wrote the history of Colwyn Bay, and also a keen Scout leader, once confided that his greatest ambition would be to be granted an honorary degree by the University College of North Wales. Sadly, I don't think it happened, although he deserved recognition for his contribution to the cultural life of north Wales.

Each Monday I would call to see Annie Williams, the registrar, to take down the details of those who had married or died. Coverage of weddings was provided by giving the families special forms on which they could jot down the details, such as what the bride was wearing, a description of the bouquet, and where the honeymoon was spent (usually Blackpool, the Lake District or London). Then the challenge was to provide a newsy report about pretty brides carrying posies of lily of the valley, not forgetting the outfits of her mother and the bridesmaids.

These days reporters dread the 'death knock' – calling at the home of the bereaved. There are official demands, usually by the police and entirely unsolicited, for families 'to be left to grieve in privacy'. In the 1950s the call was almost a daily event for a weekly reporter composing obituaries. Far from 'intrusion', there was usually a welcome for the man from the local paper. Even, on the odd occasion, a cordial invitation to 'come and look at Harry in his coffin; he's smiling and at peace now'. In those days the body would lie in a parlour or bedroom until the funeral.

Once, I attended the funeral of a local 'worthy', and afterwards stood outside Llanelian Church taking down the names of every mourner – and there were more than a hundred. This wasn't merely training for journalism, but for life.

Contacts, contacts, contacts. That was the name of the game. A list of people to be phoned or visited weekly or daily. Each vicar or minister of religion was likely to receive a personal call, and usually my transport would be a bike. The Rotary Club, Inner Wheel, and Soroptimists could all rely on their activities being recorded. Ratepayers' Associations were a great source of news. I was even sent to a weekly meeting of the Colwyn Bay Spiritualist Society – 'for experience'.

Then, later, I was to be entrusted with courts and councils. Courts were once a fortnight, councils once a month at night, members giving their services free. I remember my first inquest, a gory story about death in an overturned car. That cured me of squeamishness.

After a holiday in London I was impressed by 'Star Man's Diary', a gossip column in *The Star*, a great evening paper later to be closed quite unnecessarily. I called my column 'Pioneer Man's Diary', filling it with gossip and opinion. (Sometimes too much opinion. I've always been opinionated!)

Football, too, became an important part of life. I had to fill the sports page each week, both with reports on Colwyn Bay's activities in the Welsh League (North) and a column called 'Bay Jottings', presenting all the gossip.

Each Saturday afternoon I would watch Colwyn Bay at home, or travel with the team in their coach to such exotic sporting fields as those in Holyhead, Blaenau Ffestiniog,

Bethesda, Pwllheli, Porthmadog, Flint, Holywell and, when it wasn't under water, Llanrwst.

If there were two events or matches at the same time there would be an arrangement with the reporter on the *Weekly News*, the tiny, humorous and talented Trevor Williams, whose sporting title was 'Cormorant'. We would provide 'blacks' (carbon copies) for each other.

Colwyn Bay had a good team in those days, with former league professionals taking the opportunity for a few pounds a week to turn out for the club, or maybe for a full-time job with a local engineering firm whose managing director was club president. One member of the team was Bill Lawton, husband of actress Dora Bryan, who was also a league cricketer as well as a fine wing-half.

Each Friday evening I spent an hour at the home of Archie Woodiwiss, a council clerk and shorthand expert. He would teach me the intricacies of Pitman's, including the great outline which was his own surname, and finally I got my certificate for achieving 120 words a minute. Being a reporter without shorthand is like having a hand behind your back. It was to save me a thousand times.

I learned about the importance of the affinity between a local paper and its town. It was a relationship which sadly has been destroyed in recent years. In so many cases journalism has been dismantled by closing offices and sacking staff, including local editors.

Reports about forthcoming films would be written up with the aid of greatly exaggerated propaganda provided by companies and cinemas. Each Monday night, summer and winter, there would be two free seats at the Colwyn Bay Repertory Theatre.

In those days, pre-TV, the theatre would often be full. Actresses, and there were some very pretty ones, were usually free of rehearsals on Thursday afternoons, and like us had complimentary seats at the cinemas. Could life be more perfect?

In summer there were variety shows at the Pier Pavilion covered on a Tuesday. Stars like Ken Dodd, Morecambe and Wise and Harry Secombe cut their teeth there. On Sunday evenings there would be a 'celebrity concert' with the Pier Orchestra (conducted by Charles Haberreiter) and leading classical singers. Another 'perk' was reviewing records, mostly 78s. I called myself 'Discus'. My unkind sister suggested it was short for Disgusting! What better gift though, to impress a girlfriend than the voice of Hutch singing a classic from *High Society*?

I got my introduction to politics, but more of this later. I was also introduced to strong liquor. Not quite 18, I enjoyed a St David's Day dinner at the Rhos Abbey Hotel, Rhos-on-Sea, with colleague Trevor Williams and a photographer, Joffre Cull. Many glasses of wine were consumed. I sat in the photographer's battered car for the journey home and the door flew open on Colwyn Bay promenade. I thought I was hallucinating. Trevor couldn't stop laughing...

There was a fortnight's holiday each year. Time off was rare. But in a job like that, who needed a holiday? In Llandudno stars of a film called *The Card*, based on Arnold Bennett's book, arrived for the premiere. Among them was the lovely Petula Clark who autographed her photograph. The drinks were mainly gin and Italian. When I got back to the office I couldn't stop talking. Luckily that's about the main effect that drink used to have on me, talking too much. Nowadays I'm close to teetotal.

4

Serving the Queen – by order!

OF COURSE IT couldn't last. Utopia had to end. It did so one day when calling-up papers arrived. I had enjoyed a year's deferment so that I could perfect my shorthand, but the moment had come.

Most of my pals joined the RAF or found themselves in the Royal Welch Fusiliers. One was in the Royal Army Ordnance Corps and had a wonderful posting to NATO headquarters in Paris, where he wore civilian clothes. Another friend saw out his two years in the West Indies. But I had to be different. When I presented myself at the recruiting office in Wrexham for my medical (passed A1!), I opted for two years in the Royal Navy. A naval lieutenant explained that all the National Service vacancies had been filled. However, I could get into the Royal Marines, 'the next best thing'.

I had heard very little about the Royal Marines. He assured me that I'd do some initial training, then be posted, probably, to an aircraft carrier, do a few enjoyable voyages around the Mediterranean, and that would be it. I was a naive young man, and he was telling whoppers. I got a clue when, back in Colwyn Bay, my pal Gwyn Jones told me: 'Royal Marines, that's pretty tough, Derek. What have you done?' How right he was. As for impressing the girls, the only person attracted to my 'blues' was to be an elderly gay at Paddington station as I waited for a train to Plymouth one night!

When I presented myself at Lympstone Infantry Training Centre, near Exeter, I got a shock. Instead of travelling overnight I'd made a single day's journey of it, arriving at 6 p.m. when the latest reporting time was 4 p.m. My mother was determined that I should not devote a single extra hour to Queen and Country! 'Not a very good start, lad,' barked a major as I gathered my bedding. Somehow life didn't seem to be so promising.

The next three months were the biggest culture change a young man from a sheltered background, such as myself, could suffer. Climbing ropes with full kit, swinging Tarzan-like from trees, running up and down hillsides, the assault course, the dreaded 'Death Slide' – sliding down a rope at 45 degrees clutching a 'toggle' which was placed round it – sleeping in holes dug in the ground, firing rifles, Sten guns, Bren guns, bazookas, mortars, throwing grenades, sleeping overnight in Sidmouth Gasworks, then rendezvousing at 6 a.m. on the local golf course. A bigger change from the life of pleasure and indulgence I'd led in Colwyn Bay would be hard to find. Marching, shining buttons, extra parades, peeling spuds...

Three months later came the passing-out parade. The drill colour sergeant told us: 'You are now trained killers.' That was not something of which I was particularly proud or mentioned to my mother! Our squad – No. 823 – then progressed to the Commando School in Bickleigh on the edge of Dartmoor. Only the kit went the full distance. Halfway there we were told to get out of the truck – and walk the rest of the way.

Yet Bickleigh, despite its reputation, proved easy. I was so fit after the three months of enforced purgatory at Lympstone that I was prepared for anything, and that included rock climbing (sometimes at night), more live firing, and a 30-mile map march across Dartmoor. Once, camped out on the moor in bitter mid November, the tent blew down. We could see the lights of the prison and I remember thinking that at least those inside were warm.

Discipline was tough. On parade one Saturday morning

after a particularly gruelling spell on Dartmoor, the inspecting officer asked me to remove my right boot. Knowing I had a hole in my sock, I removed the left. He continued down the ranks then returned to me, and was not fooled. 'I said the right boot,' he barked. Seeing my bare heel meant being confined to camp that day – and missing a soccer trip to watch Plymouth Argyle.

In one of his books Paddy Ashdown, a former marine, recalled being puzzled about why, on exercises, three pieces of toilet paper were issued as part of the kit. A crusty sergeant major had replied to his question: 'One up, one down, one to polish, lad.'

There was 'the regain'. This involved crawling on top of a rope across a fast-flowing river. A physical training instructor would shake the rope so you slipped beneath, having to use elbow and leg to regain your position. I was actually hanging off the rope by my arms but was not prepared to drop into the river, the tradition being that if you did so you raised a salute before hitting the deep water. By a superhuman effort I swung a leg back on to the rope and hauled myself up. To this day I don't know how I summoned the strength.

Our final test was a nine-mile speed march with full kit. To me 'yomping', as it became known later, was not a problem. But my proudest moment in the Royal Marines was carrying my rifle and also that of the squad loudmouth who moaned in agony as I helped him across the finishing line after the trek which marked the end of the course. The green beret awaited, presented by the colonel. Then it was home for a fortnight's Christmas leave. Typically, Christmas leave was combined with embarkation leave.

In January 1953, after spending the night on a bunk deep in a station on the London underground used as a pre-embarkation point, I flew to Malta aboard an ancient Viking aircraft which had to land in Nice to refuel. In Malta I was told I would be joining 45 Commando, which was training in Tripoli. After an overnight stay in a Nissen hut in Luqa airport, I flew to Libya aboard an RAF Dakota, landing at Idris airfield, named after the then monarch.

I joined 45 Commando at Tarhuna, a training camp in the desert which presented a scene reminiscent of the film *Beau Geste*. The locals had commandeered the doors and windows, and we lay on stretchers on the floor. Sometimes desert dogs would stroll in, lick our faces as we lay asleep, then be sent scampering with shouts and curses. Once, on guard at night, I was surrounded by a pack of them in the galley (cookhouse). I stood still and thankfully they went away.

We went on exercises deep into the desert and tried to hide from the RAF, trekking miles through wadis.

Intrepid cliff climbers scaled the flagpole mounted on an obelisk to fly the unit flag. Because I had shorthand and typing I had a job in the orderly room, but for the rest of the time was just an ordinary general duties marine fulfilling all the menial tasks and guard duties.

Tarhuna was an intriguing barracks. Only ten years before, during the Second World War, it had been used as a staging post for British POWs. On the walls was graffiti from that time. I can still remember, 'Hard luck, Joe, RIP, Royal Northumberland Fusiliers,' or 'Sorry You Didn't Make It Tom,' or, more cheerfully and hopefully, 'See you back in Blighty – One Day.' It seemed that most had been Geordies.

For the first time in my life I had a boil – a giant one in the middle of my forehead. It was probably due to perspiration beneath the green beret when struggling up and down wadis. I reported sick. The Royal Navy medic offered me his wisdom. 'Know where you've gone wrong, Lofty?' he asked. Anxious to receive his advice, I replied that I had no idea. 'You shouldn't have joined,' he grinned.

Our regimental sergeant major (RSM) had served in the famed Long Range Desert Group during the war, until his capture. In Tripoli he'd been abused by the locals as he was put on a prison ship bound for Italy.

In the spring of 1953, as we left Tripoli on the landing ships

Reggio and *Dieppe*, returning to Malta, it couldn't have been more different. They cheered us, called us 'Effendi' ('Sir') – and offered us their wares.

Soon we were at St Patrick's Barracks, Malta. Each morning the Royal Marines band played 'The Dashing White Sergeant'. A strange thing had happened. I had begun to enjoy my new life.

5

Heat and sand

MALTA IN APRIL and May was idyllic. There was a good social life, with meals down 'The Gut' – the infamous Strait Street which really, in that overwhelmingly Roman Catholic country, was tame despite its reputation for sin.

There were dances at the NAAFI club at Floriana, attractive dark-haired girls, one in particular called Rose. At Sliema submarines and frigates of the British Mediterranean Fleet were the backdrop. One day Tito of Yugoslavia arrived aboard his presidential yacht.

However, our stay was short-lived. In Egypt there was trouble. King Farouk had been deposed and a militant young officer called Neguib had taken over. British troops were becoming a target and the situation was getting dangerous. Cue, of course, the Royal Marines.

We sailed that May in a converted submarine depot ship called HMS *Ranpura*, at a steady few knots across the Mediterranean. To pass the time, Oerlikon guns were fired at targets in the sea. It was beginning to get hot, and shirts were off. For me that was a great mistake. When I walked down the gangplank in Port Said with a Bergen rucksack on my back and rifle across my shoulder, my flesh was pillar-box red. I had to grin and bear it, for to report sick would have invited a charge. For nearly a week my skin peeled in agony!

From Port Said we were taken by truck to a tented camp in the desert near Geneifa. Life became interminable guard duty. I spent Coronation Day guarding families at a camp alongside the Great Bitter Lake. Often we would see the French liner *Pasteur* pass through, reputed to touch the bottom sometimes as she sailed across.

Several times we moved camp, each time under canvas in the sand. Once, most of us caught dysentery and the unit was isolated. Soldiers in trucks passing our camp yelled 'Unclean' in ridicule. Then it was to Port Fouad, directly across the harbour from Port Said, where we were to stay in tents for the rest of my time in Egypt. It was named after a royal dynasty.

The night-time guard duty continued. The scariest was at the railway marshalling yards at Port Said, where every shadow or noise jangled the nerves. However the most exhilarating was guarding the ammunition trains running for nearly a hundred miles through the night to Tel El Kebir, which had the reputation of being the biggest munitions base in the world. We literally rode shotgun, perched in an open truck from which we got a full view of the train. A memory which will remain forever is a moonlit night, desert, and a ship with all its lights on emerging suddenly along the canal, as if an apparition in the sand.

In the weary early hours an Egyptian railway foreman invited us to 'leave your weapons and have a cup of tea' at a junction where we stopped. No thanks! A few weeks later a Royal Engineer was killed there.

My luckiest escape was in a Land Rover on the road alongside the canal, on escort duty. The crack of a rifle shot resonated above our heads. 'Drive on,' ordered the corporal. In any case it would have been impossible to find the sniper. As Winston Churchill once said: 'Nothing in life is so exhilarating as to be shot at without result.' In a year our unit lost four men, two of them when they were driven off that road. The padre was one of those who escaped from the crash.

On manoeuvres beside the Red Sea we dug bivouacs in the sand for the night. At 7 a.m. there was an inspection of weapons. RSM Rendell chose to inspect the barrel of my .303 rifle. It was gleaming. 'If you can do it in the sand lad, then so should everyone else,' said the RSM approvingly. I felt a twinge of guilt because I'd inserted wire wool with the pull-through – a trick that was strictly forbidden.

I had a lot of time for RSM Rendell. Each time a new draft arrived from the UK, distinguished by their white knees, he would speak to them. He'd say to the young lads fresh from training: 'What's the first thing you'll do tonight? I'll tell you – you're going to write to your mum and tell her you're all right, because she'll be worrying about you.' No phone call home in those days!

A memory of Port Fouad was an Egyptian tailor and laundry man – or 'dhobi wallah' – allowed to operate from a tent within the camp. When ironing a pair of tropical trousers or a shirt he would first take a gulp of water from a mug, then spit it out in a spray where the creases were to be.

On 1 March 1954 the adjutant, Captain John Owen, came into our tent quietly and presented me with a half bottle of whisky 'to celebrate St David's Day'. I shared it with my pals. Captain Owen had joined the Marines during the war, saw service in the Far East, then left to become a London policeman. But soon he was back, serving in Malaya. He was an officer everyone looked up to – and he rose to become Major General.

In May 1954 I said goodbye to the Canal Zone, its heat and flies and with not too many regrets. My biggest was not being able to see a single pyramid, or visit Cairo – all out of bounds from the Canal Zone which we protected. The nearest I got to Cairo was to see its lights glowing in the sky many miles away during a desert exercise. I sailed from Port Said to Malta on the light cruiser HMS *Delight*, one of a new class which sped through the Mediterranean, unlike our journey in the opposite direction aboard the *Ranpura*. I had two heavy kitbags bearing all my service possessions. Typically, already being laden, I was given a Bren gun to carry as well.

In Malta life returned for a few weeks to what it had been like a year previously. And, surprise, I was invited to RSM

Rendell's home for a meal with his wife and children – and he insisted on Christian names!

I was with a group who had returned to the George Cross island to parade for the Queen and Prince Philip during their coronation tour of the Commonwealth. It was a glorious, sunny day on the parade ground in Floriana... bands playing, colours flying, Richard Dimbleby commentating.

Then, a few days before my 21st birthday and sister Joan's wedding, it was back to Britain. An RAF Dakota landed in Croydon after an eight-hour flight. After emerging unscathed from customs, with a few watches brought home as gifts for pals' girlfriends, I put in a reverse charge call to Colwyn Bay. I spoke to my parents and sister for the first time in 17 months.

With typical official stupidity, I first had to report to Stonehouse Barracks in Plymouth before starting my six weeks' demob leave, taking a train through the night. They wanted to know if I was due any dental treatment or had handed in library books before I could catch that train to Colwyn Bay.

After leave, it was back to the Napoleonic barracks in Plymouth. There came the day that I walked out for the last time. For Marine (First Class) Bellis, RM129728, who had never fired a gun in anger, it was over – well, nearly.

A year later, during a Suez crisis, I was one of the 'Z Men' recalled for a month's training, just in case. Luckily I had retained my uniform. The training was in June, in sunny Portsmouth. It passed quickly, and the nightlife was great. I got paid by the Marines and by the *Northants Evening Telegraph*, so there was plenty of cash to spend in Southsea. I never wore my uniform again.

Some years ago I joined the north Wales branch of the Royal Marines Association and became secretary for six years. One reason I joined was to help and recognise the courage of those bootnecks who served in Afghanistan and Iraq, as well as to enjoy the social life. It's the biggest fundraising organisation to which I've ever belonged, raising £11,000 in a year, mainly because of elderly ex-Marines standing in the foyers of north Wales supermarkets with their green berets and medals – and collecting tins. Now I've resigned as secretary, passing on the mantle to younger blood.

I've just come across my Royal Marines service certificate. It says that my efficiency was 'Satisfactory', character 'VG'. That was superior to 'Good', 'Fair', 'Indifferent' or 'Bad'!

6

North Wales –
Northants – Merseyside

ON RETURN FROM National Service, I spent six more months on the *Pioneer*. It was as pleasant as before but I was ambitious and wanted to move on to greater things. I used to study what experts wrote, and sometimes adopted expressions I found in *The Stage* to describe concerts and plays. I also supplied *The Stage* with 'notices' when a premiere was performed at the Repertory Theatre – and was paid seven shillings and sixpence a time.

I covered a trial at Ruthin Assizes of a man who was cleared of murder after a fight in the street. There was medical evidence which was beyond my understanding as various doctors gave their findings. But it was not above the comprehension of Evan Williams, a former war correspondent and north Wales man for the *Daily Dispatch*. 'GP says Dr Grace is wrong,' declared the headline next morning. Evan Williams had digested ALL the evidence and realised that Geoffrey Evans, a popular Colwyn Bay GP, was contradicting the expert evidence of Dr William Grace, a world-renowned Home Office pathologist. He was the first of many great reporters I was to meet.

I applied for a job on the *Evening Telegraph* in Wellingborough, but turned it down because I wanted more money. Back came a telegram saying my wish was granted. I had a few regrets leaving the comfortable and enjoyable life in Colwyn Bay. My 'digs', the first in my life, were with a Congregational minister – the Rev. Lionel Willoughby and his wonderful family. Sometimes, after a convivial night, I would walk the streets until their lights had gone out!

I started work in Wellingborough in January 1955 and remained there and at nearby Kettering for a year. The training was brilliant – supplying both a lively evening paper and a weekly. The evening paper could take news until 4.30 in the afternoon, when Stop Press items were provided by teleprinter. Yet now, in the days of the internet and incredible technology, the deadline for the print edition of most evening papers is – the night before!

The *Evening Telegraph* had a wonderful editor called Ray Parkin. He read every word in the paper. Parkin compiled a style book and one day sent a memo to all editorial staff saying he'd spent some time studying the length of 'intros' (the first paragraph of a story) and found them to be too wordy. Then came advice which I have tried to follow throughout my writing career. 'Please remember,' wrote Parkin, 'that we have an inexhaustible supply of full stops.' I still have his style book.

Again, contacts were the lifeblood of our journalism. One colleague started every morning with the call 'Good morning, bishop' – speaking to a bishop who had retired from an African diocese to Northamptonshire. Our police contacts were excellent too, particularly because a young woman colleague was a niece of an Inspector of Constabulary. When the local inspector realised that, he was a changed man.

Each Monday we would have a ticket for lunch with Wellingborough Rotarians. As a reporter in those days you knew everyone and little happened without you finding out. There were human interest stories aplenty.

A woman assaulted by a GI based locally explained to me how he'd thrust a knife near her breast. 'Show 'im Renee,' said her sister, and she presented her large scarred boob for my inspection.

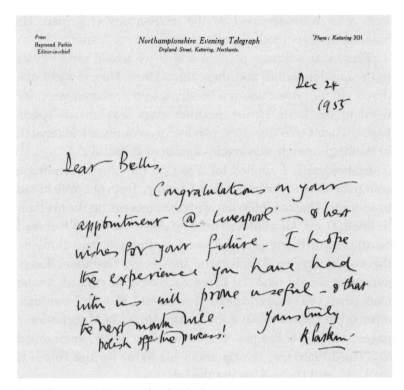

From
Raymond Parkin
Editor-in-chief

Northamptonshire Evening Telegraph
Dryland Street, Kettering, Northants.

'Phone: Kettering 3131

Ray Parkin – great editor, great handwriting!

In the *Wellingborough News*, a weekly we also serviced, I visited the homes of poor families at Christmas and wrote such an emotional piece I was certain that offers of cash and presents would flood into the office. Alas, the sole response was a ten-shilling note – from a reader in South Africa.

At Northamptonshire Assizes (this was before legal aid), a thief with no money and no barrister was offered what was called a 'dock brief' – he had merely to point at the lawyer he wished to represent him and his services would be provided free. He pointed at the one man not allowed to do so – one of Britain's most famous and expensive QCs, engaged in a fraud case.

It was also in Northampton that I saw my first miscarriage of justice. It involved a man accused of a sex offence whose story was misunderstood by the magistrates' chairman. He mistook his hypothetical explanation for a confession.

There was a 'linage pool' in which we would send stories to the London dailies and share the takings. How proud I was that a story of mine about a beauty queen appeared word for word in the *Daily Mirror*. Another story was on the sports pages, when Colin Cowdrey, playing in a county cricket match in Wellingborough, was made captain of England.

Emboldened, I applied for a job on the *Mirror*, sending a colourful letter to the boss, Hugh Cudlipp, 'from one Welshman to another'. I had an interview with the news editor, the brilliant Kenneth Hord. All went well until he asked me what I had read on the train. Being of a left wing inclination, and thinking this would impress, I replied the *Manchester Guardian*. 'Every journalist should read the *Times* each day,' he rapped. 'Come back when you're a little older.' I never did, though I was later offered but turned down a job on the *Mirror* in Manchester. I passed on to a colleague of mine in Manchester, summoned to a Hord interview, the tip about his liking for the *Times*. It worked – and Harry King got the job.

That summer I met Glyn Rees, the great news editor of the *Liverpool Daily Post*. A few months later he offered me the job of district reporter in Wallasey for the *Daily Post and Echo*, which I accepted.

Glyn was a news editor of the style which, regrettably, will never be seen again. On his desk he had a diary the size of a family Bible on which every upcoming event and story which needed covering was noted. If, for instance, a court case was adjourned, the date of the new hearing would be written down and it would be covered automatically.

I used to think how lucky I was to be receiving a few pounds above the minimum rate in my wages, collected each Friday night in cash from the office in Victoria Street, Liverpool. However, I was in fact doing the work of TWO reporters – starting at 8 a.m. with stories for the *Echo*, then at 4 p.m. beginning work all over again for the *Daily Post*. Sometimes

THE LIVERPOOL DAILY POST AND ECHO LTD.

LIVERPOOL DAILY POST.   LIVERPOOL ECHO.

A. G. JEANS
ASSISTANT MANAGING DIRECTOR

VICTORIA STREET,
LIVERPOOL, I.

21st December 1955.

H. D. Bellis, Esq.,
c/o 20 Hatton Avenue,
WELLINGBOROUGH,
Northants.

Dear Mr. Bellis,

Thank you for your letter. I remember you at
the time I was interviewing people for one of the North
Wales reporting positions.

I am now able to offer you a position as district
reporter in Wallasey as a member of the Birkenhead,
Wallasey and Wirral team. The salary would be the
rate for your age in a city the size of Liverpool. I am
unable to be more specific because there has not yet
been any announcement of the new scale arranged
between the Newspaper Society and the journalists'
organisations about which ballots are being held. I
think the rate for your age would be about £10:6:3.

The duties would be representing our morning
and evening paper in the self-contained borough of
Wallasey and thus all the normal duties of a district

continued ...

Daily Post appointment letter, 1955

council meetings in Wallasey Town Hall, conducted on bitter
party lines, would last till nearly midnight.

Derek Taylor took care of the adjoining 'patch' of Wirral.
We would cover for each other on days off. Derek always
managed this when Heswall Council held their meetings, so I
would go by bus from Birkenhead to cover. There was method
in his choice of day off – because Heswall was the home of

Alick Jeans, whose family ran the *Post and Echo*, and a near-verbatim report was required.

Later Derek was to join me on the *News Chronicle* in Manchester, after which he did showbiz for the *Express*. And after that he travelled worldwide as Press officer for the Beatles. Another young journalist learning his trade on the *Post and Echo* and showing talent which would drive him to the top was Gordon Reece, later to serve the Conservative Party and Mrs Thatcher with great distinction.

They were great days on Merseyside, where I stayed for two and a half years. Major stories, too, with murders, trials, collisions in the foggy Mersey, river rescues off New Brighton.

Once, a man and wife who drowned when their yacht overturned in the Irish Sea were swept by the tide into the River Mersey, their wrists lashed together with rope. In death, they wanted to be together.

I covered an hilarious trial in which it was denied a local house was being run as a brothel for the benefit of American servicemen based at Burtonwood, near Warrington. A GI insisted that the woman in bed with him when the police burst in was his fiancée, and certainly not a prostitute. What's her name? he was asked. 'Joan,' he replied. And her surname? 'Just Joan to me, Sir!'

One Saturday at 7 a.m. I went aboard a liner to interview the chairman of the Wales Tourist Board, Huw T. Edwards, on his return from a tourist-boosting trip to Canada.

I was in the office in Liverpool on the day of the city carnival (sponsored by the *Echo*) when a Hungarian 'human bird' leapt from a plane intending to fly to Earth. Alas, the wings didn't work and he crashed to his death, watched by horrified photographers in the Dakota.

Alick Jeans would sometimes jot a line of congratulations on a story well done and announce a pay rise to show his appreciation. He ran a tight ship but that family ownership was tough but fair, so preferable to what we have today. He believed in journalism, even though sometimes he would demand that his personal foibles be indulged. The greatest of these was his dislike of nationalisation – British Railways in particular. Every Friday some unfortunate reporter would trudge to Lime Street and obtain the arrival times of all the London expresses that week. Inevitably the headlines would be something like 'Another bad week for the Merseyside Express'. Reporters used to joke that it was all because Jeans' father had never bought him a Hornby model train when he was a lad.

Periodically Jeans would call meetings of all his district reporters. He produced a league table of 'boxes' – paragraphs that appeared in the Stop Press column of the *Echo*. Working in busy Wallasey I had no difficulty in finding plenty.

I had my introduction to the Press Gallery at the House of Commons when I covered the passage of the Wallasey Corporation Bill.

One night, I was sent to cover the annual dinner of the Wirral Tory Party, an event I didn't relish because I'd had a painful visit to the dentist that day. Selwyn Lloyd, the local MP and Foreign Secretary, tried to take a rise out of the media during his speech. First, he asked if there was a journalist present. I put my hand up, being the only one there, and said I was representing the *Daily Post*. He asked me not to report what he was about to say.

THE LIVERPOOL DAILY POST AND ECHO LTD.
LIVERPOOL DAILY POST   LIVERPOOL ECHO

FROM
A. G. JEANS   VICTORIA STREET
ASSISTANT MANAGING DIRECTOR   LIVERPOOL 1

Personal   21st March 1957.

Mr. H. D. Bellis,
Wallasey.

I have much pleasure in increasing your salary by 15s. a week
from 10th March 1957.

Big money coming my way in 1957!

45

Then he joked about how he fooled cameramen and reporters outside No. 10 who had been expecting him to be sacked after the Suez fiasco (and he should have lost his job, because he hid the truth about collusion with the French and Israelis). He described, to laughter from his fawning followers, how he had 'practised' in the mirror, feigning a glum face before leaving No. 10 to infer he'd been fired. To keep my word, I didn't report what he had said – in the *Daily Post*, anyway. I told my friend Tim Leuty on the then *Sunday Pictorial* instead!

Liverpool had a famous Press Club. Most of the national papers had two reporters as well as a staff photographer based in the city, and it was at the Club that they spent their days and nights and did their work. When a major story broke, one of the reporters would provide the cover – and share it with the rest. Some news desks, particularly the *Daily Mail*, tried to break 'the ring' – but none succeeded. This was at a time when an arsonist was setting fire to ships, when stones were thrown at a bishop in the street, and when Liverpool was one of the busiest news centres in the country.

THE LIVERPOOL DAILY POST AND ECHO LTD.
LIVERPOOL DAILY POST   LIVERPOOL ECHO

FROM
A. G. JEANS   VICTORIA STREET
MANAGING DIRECTOR
AND   LIVERPOOL 1
EDITOR-IN-CHIEF

5th June, 1958.

Mr. H.D. Bellis,
42, Coniston Avenue,
Wallasey, Cheshire.

On my return I have your letter giving notice to take effect on 20th June and telling me that you are going to the News Chronicle.

I am glad you have enjoyed your time with us and wish you every success in the future.

Alick Jeans

Leaving for pastures new, 1958

The social life on Merseyside was wonderful. Each Friday night after collecting wages, everyone would assemble in the New Court Bar for drinks. My landlady was Selina Highet, a remarkable woman who was the widow of the Wallasey coroner. She treated me like a son.

Each week night at Reece's Restaurant there would be dances on two floors. One summer night I met a tall and stunning nurse called Shirley. I bought her a drink while I spent 20 minutes on the phone, dictating copy. She didn't mind too much – and the rest is history. Just over a year later we were married – and in later years SHE phoned my copy! She also bore me three sons and two daughters. We've just celebrated our diamond wedding with all our children and grandchildren present, including Nigel from Los Angeles. We have been blessed! Now we have our first great-grandchild, Florence Bellis.

7

Life in the 'Fleet Street of the north'

I'D VOWED TO be working on a national paper by the time I was 24, and I just made it. I joined the *News Chronicle*, that staid and respectable organ of the Liberal Party, at their offices in Manchester – not far from Strangeways jail. There were some great journalists on that paper, including the veteran Whitney Rowland. I remember bow-tied Whitney, who enjoyed snuff, telling me how once he'd covered a famous murder case in which a judge told a woman, subsequently reprieved, that she needn't listen to the death sentence because it wouldn't apply in her case. Then he put on the black cap and pronounced the dreaded words in a whisper.

My first job for them was a menial task covering the northern final of the Lorry Driver of the Year competition, which the paper was sponsoring at Maine Road football ground.

More exciting stories were to follow. In August 1959 I flew to Bantry Bay in Ireland to meet Commander Victor Clark, who in six years had sailed 48,000 miles around the world in a 20ft ketch called *Solace*. It was an exclusive story which led the paper, and I got a telegram of congratulations from the editor in London.

The *Daily Mail* turned up but, believing, wrongly, that we had paid him a great deal of money – I didn't discourage that belief – they disappeared. Commander Clark was a hero with two Distinguished Service Crosses, had commanded a destroyer at Narvik, was torpedoed in the battleship *Repulse*, led a guerrilla band in Malaya, then after a motor launch was blown up beneath him he spent three years as a prisoner of the Japanese. Yet still he craved more adventure!

A month later I was in Bolton where Field Marshal Earl Montgomery faced a Labour boycott. He'd made a remark about 'barmy Labour voters', so 48 small-minded aldermen and councillors wouldn't join him for lunch. Monty, the hero of Alamein, laughed the night before: 'I am the only living freeman of Bolton. Whether Bolton will have a LIVING freeman or not tomorrow...'

In May 1960 I was with 65,000 at Maine Road football ground, covering the crowd scenes when Burnley beat

Monty jokes about Labour boycott

N.C. 13 OCT 1959

By DEREK BELLIS

FIELD-MARSHAL EARL MONT-GOMERY, who faces a Labour boycott at Bolton today because of his election remark about "barmy" Labour voters, told a Manchester school's pupils and their parents last night:

"I am the only living freeman of Bolton. Whether Bolton will have a *living* freeman or not tomorrow . . ." The rest of his words were drowned in laughter and applause.

Monty, who was presenting the prizes at the 300-year-old Chetham's Hospital, told parents he wanted to say something to the boys.

NO POLITICS

"Let me know if you don't approve of what I say," he added to the parents. "Let me know. Which, of course, some people occasionally do."

Then he went on: "I can't be accused tonight of making a political speech. I probably will be—but it won't be right."

Two members of the 50-strong Labour group on Bolton Town Council have been given a "dispensation" so that they may attend the lunch to mark the 10th anniversary of Lord Montgomery's election as a freeman of the Borough.

They are Councillor Alan Brigg

Monty congratulates Basil Hewitt, winner of Chetham's Hospital Montgomery Prize.

and Councillor Mrs. Elsie Bocock, both of whom work at mills which Monty will visit.

'AN INSULT'

"I did not wish to be discourteous to my employers who, after all, are Monty's hosts in the afternoon," said Councillor Brigg.

But the remaining 48 Labour aldermen and councillors will not be at the lunch.

Alderman James Vickers, World War I Service man and a former

mayor, who announced the boycott, said they believed Monty's remark—even though he has apologised for it and said it was intended as a joke—to be "an insult to the intelligence and integrity of nearly half of the electorate.

"It portrays a thoroughly unchivalrous attitude to millions of ex-Service men who have fought and suffered in war for the ideals of democratic government."

The leader of the council's Conservatives, Councillor Alfred Hutchinson, commented: "We have been called a lot of nasty names such as 'vermin' and 'beasts' which I think are more abusive than Montgomery's. People who used these expressions have not apologised, but Monty has.

"I think I would have accepted the apology and let bygones be bygones."

REPLANNED

Now today's lunch has been replanned for 60 guests instead of 100 as originally intended.

Monty read of the boycott after a visit to Manchester Grammar School. He said to his host, Mr. William Mather, of Whirley Hall, Macclesfield, Cheshire:

"Well, I've made an apology. I can't do anything more."

Snub for Monty, 1959

Manchester City 2–1 to become First Division soccer champions. To celebrate, the £20-a-week heroes drank sherry from teacups in the dressing room with their chairman, the butcher Bob Lord, then one of the most controversial men in football.

Coverage of conferences wasn't easy because they usually involved providing enough copy to fill an entire page for a special 'slip' edition sent to the host town. So whether it was Alf Robens with an unwelcome master plan to drag the Co-operative movement into the 1960s, or a National Union of Teachers' conference being sweet-talked by an education minister, it was hard work.

The Co-operative Union was a favourite conference because journalists always received a generous gift – a canteen of cutlery in my case. In Fleetwood I was the only man at the Women Liberals' conference where Mrs Grimond, wife of the leader Jo, was president. In recognition of my efforts for the ladies I was presented with a tea towel.

In York I covered the Convocation of Bishops, presided over by Archbishop Ramsey, and discovered that some bishops really do go to sleep during debates.

And it was back to Fleetwood for a case in which a deckhand got three months and three others were fined (as much as £35!) for a drunken New Year's Day mutiny aboard a trawler.

My next trip to Ireland was to write about the Irish Army achieving its 'manhood', with 600 of its troops going to join a UN contingent in the Congo. Then I was diverted to write a piece about the 'free airport of Shannon', a duty-free industrial complex adjoining the airport where a Japanese firm called Sony had started to assemble transistor radios for export to America.

I stayed the night in a hut at the end of the runway – to be rudely awoken at 4 a.m. when airliners touched down after their flights across the Atlantic. In those days, of course, they were powered by propellers, which meant that flights across the 'pond' had to land in Shannon to refuel.

Eire troops rush to join Congo draft

N.C. 21 JUL 1960

By DEREK BELLIS

THEY were smiling proudly in Dublin last night—happy that an Army has reached its manhood.

That is the reaction throughout Eire to the news that 600 of its soldiers are flying to join the United Nations forces in the Congo.

It is a far cry from those days in 1922 when the first recruits joined the newly formed Free State Army. The "uniform" then was slouch hats and dirty raincoats.

But now the 7,000-strong Eire Army—it has one officer for 10 men—is claimed to be a highly disciplined, efficient force, although the defence budget is the smallest in Western Europe.

The only thing it lacks, and here it is almost unique among modern armies, is fighting experience. It has never been on active service at home or abroad. Never has it fired a shot in anger.

In Jerusalem

Of the 9,000 in the Eire armed forces, including the Air Corps and Naval Service, exactly 52, all officers, have seen service abroad. Fifty of them were rushed to the Lebanon to act as United Nations observers in 1958 and two others are doing the same job in Jerusalem.

For some of the troops a pilgrimage to Lourdes has been the furthest venture from home.

Small wonder that yesterday hundreds of soldiers were besieging their commanding officers with requests to be on this weekend's Congo draught.

The battalion, a self-contained force of a headquarters company and three companies of infantry groups, will be armed with British rifles and Bren guns, Swedish sub-machine guns and French light mortars.

The Commanding Officer, it was announced last night, will be 45-year-old Lieutenant Colonel Mortimer Buckley, married with seven children, of Killarney, County Kerry.

Tall, dark haired and ruddy complexioned, he enlisted as a cadet in 1937 and was commissioned two years later. Colonel Buckley has been an executive officer with the Army's Western Command.

Inoculated

The successful voluteers for this history-making detachment are all A1—and smart. Eire knows the whole army will be judged by these men.

Between now and the week-end when they will be transported in US Globemaster aircraft, the 600 will be inoculated against yellow fever and smallpox and if time permits also against polio and typhoid. They will assemble at the Curragh, the Aldershot of Eire.

The prospect of possible jungle warfare does not worry an army formed "to protect the country's neutrality," an army whose job, to date, has been a round of garrison duties, field training and putting part-time soldiers through their paces.

"We feel we shall be quite equal to the task. This is a peace operation," they say.

And perhaps, after all, it is only fitting that an army that might be said to have been born of colonial strife should help to ease the birthpains of an independent republic.

Another honour came the Army's way last night with the disclosure that Colonel Justin McCarthy has been appointed acting Chief of Staff of United Nations forces in the Middle East. He replaces the Swedish General Von Horn, who is in command in the Congo.

Eire volunteers for the Congo were officially stated yesterday to be "well in excess" of the numbers required.

Irish troops leave for the Congo, 1960

In September 1959 came a story that is still one of my favourites, because it made important people look a little silly and also showed the virtue of staying with an event until the end. It was the inauguration of the £18 million electrified rail line from Manchester Piccadilly to Crewe, celebrated with a slap-up luncheon for VIPs (but no one else) in the Midland Hotel.

Afterwards everyone assembled on Platform 9 – then it was switched to Platform 5. But there was no sign of the special train due to take Transport Minister Ernest Marples and the chairman of the British Transport Commission, Sir Brian Robertson, to Euston. Sir Brian paced the platform, puce-faced and furious. 'What's happened?' he demanded. The traffic manager told me between pursed lips: 'There will be

51

an inquiry, you needn't worry about that,' as everyone waited. After 13 minutes the train arrived – and left 21 minutes late. It turned out that there had been a mix-up at the Longsight sheds, only two miles away, and the VIP carriages had become trapped.

Railway bosses, for once, experienced what the rest of the population have to endure so often. Inevitably, as with so many railway stories, it brought out the 'Mr Porter' song.

My version was:

Oh, Mr Porter
What shall I do?
I'm stuck at Piccadilly
And I want to go to Crewe.

Oh dear! Only two of us were there for the story, myself and the legendary Harold Pendlebury of the *Daily Mail*. The others abandoned it earlier. I met Harold's grandson, now a *Mail* features writer, in Colwyn Bay many years later.

There were train and air crashes, murders, mysteries, and human stories. The night shift from 9 p.m. to 4 a.m. involved being the 'long-stop', often chasing the exclusives which appeared in the early editions of other nationals. There were 'the calls', a round of the major police, fire and ambulance stations in Manchester and Salford. Often a great deal of the night would be spent gossiping in the pub, until a call came from the office.

One night a reporter who had imbibed too much got in his car to do the 'calls' – then collapsed at the police station in Platt Lane. Among some reporters, a drink-driving conviction became almost the norm. An attractive and refined young woman reporter after her shift got a lift home aboard one of the newspaper delivery trucks in the early hours, and was questioned by a policeman who thought she was a lady of the night.

Then there was a flight from Manchester to Heathrow

aboard the aircraft bringing the ballerina Margot Fonteyn back from South America, where her diplomat husband had allegedly tried, without success, to organise an invasion of Panama City. I had to endure another crisis before we'd even taken off, because my young photographer (cruelly nicknamed Fairy Flashlight by the night news editor) became agitated, started to cry, and said she was too afraid to fly.

A special agency used to provide details of wills. In his, Samuel Henry Lyons, who founded Alexandre tailors, paid tribute to his wife: 'for her loving kindness and devotion and the abundance of happiness which she has given me during the whole of our married life.' Mr Lyons had to borrow sixpence for his first meal when he arrived in Leeds from Poland – but when he died 3,000 people worked for him.

In Sheffield there were the inevitable anti H-bomb protesters when the American supreme commander of NATO, General Norstad, gave a lecture. Many years later I saw his grave at Arlington cemetery, Washington DC.

One Christmas I was among a small number of journalists, magistrates and judges at Strangeways jail for the annual carol service. It was unreal. In an area of the jail known as the Rotunda was a giant Christmas tree. Photographers were allowed to take pictures of it, and, oddly, warders were over-keen to be included. (We were told by the prison authorities to call them officers, not warders, but none obliged.) In the choir was a beautiful young woman with an outstanding voice. An *Evening Chronicle* reporter recognised her as the femme fatale in a notorious crime of passion. Their headline referred to 'The Caged Nightingale'. Newspapers didn't get another invitation.

I was the chapel clerk of the National Union of Journalists. I should have smelled a rat when the management asked if we would be interested in a pension scheme. Within a month the paper had folded. Ever since, I've had a cynical view of newspaper managements.

One of the souvenirs I acquired from the *News Chronicle*

was a page proof from 'the morgue' – an obituary prepared for Winston Churchill when he was seriously ill in 1958. He lived until 1965. But the *News Chronicle* died in 1960.

8

From Manchester back to my roots

As clerk of the NUJ chapel I was dispatched to Fleet Street for the official announcement. Not only was the *News Chronicle* to be axed, with its title bought by the *Daily Mail* – was there ever such a mixture of chalk and cheese? – but the successful London evening paper, the *Star*, was closed as part of the deal. There were tears and appeals to the Cadbury family who had a financial interest in the *News Chronicle*, but to no avail. A photographer friend vowed never to eat their chocolate again. It was a bitter, sorrowful day – sadly to be repeated many times in the future. Ironically, Cadbury's itself has now been taken over.

I was one of the lucky ones. I was offered a job on the *Daily Mirror* in Manchester. But because it could not be confirmed for several days, I took the safer option of joining the reporters on the *Daily Herald*. The salary was £22 a week and, as the paper was half owned by the TUC, it was a closed shop, with membership of the NUJ mandatory.

Being of a left wing persuasion, I enjoyed my spell on the *Herald*, and in particular writing a series of features, 'Your Child at School'. It involved visiting schools all over the north-west and north Wales and little wonder it was welcomed by Fred Jarvis, spokesman of the NUT. At one school in Sheffield I was shown round by Roy Hattersley, later to become deputy leader of the Labour Party.

At Myers Grove, that city's first comprehensive, the headmaster took me into the assembly hall where a hundred earnest youngsters were taking their end-of-term exams. 'Pick out the 30 who passed the 11-plus,' he challenged.

At the end of the series I delivered my predictable verdict. Crumbling Victorian schools, not enough teachers, no (Tory) government leadership. I described headteachers as giants with their hands tied. I wonder whether the Education Minister, Sir Edward Boyle, was shown the series? My sister Joan was a schoolteacher, retiring as headmistress of Conwy Road Infants' School in Colwyn Bay. I remember her telling how at her first school in Bradford, Manchester – then one of the most industrialised square miles in Britain – she met a teacher with a magical touch. When talking to his class about Winston Churchill, a little lad interrupted rudely: 'Winston Churchill – never 'eard of 'im.' The teacher asked the boy for his name and then retorted: 'Jimmy Jones – never 'eard of 'im.' He had no more problems with that deflated lad. I've always admired charismatic teachers, because they can shape lives. Sadly we lost Joan in August 2018, a full church at the funeral on what would have been her 93rd birthday, a testament to the respect in which she was held.

For two summers I had dream assignments to cover north Wales during the August holiday period, each time taking a flat in Rhos-on-Sea, bringing the family and letting our own semi in Davyhulme, Manchester. Those were the days when sea and mountain rescues were big news. Foreign holidays had not arrived, and the area was submerged in tourists. Strangely, Friday afternoons were always the busiest, as if holidaymakers threw all caution to the wind (sometimes quite literally) when they went into the sea.

The so-called Free Wales Army was active and there were explosions at reservoirs. After a tip from a detective, I broke the story of a Welsh rancher, who made his fortune in Colombia, pledging his support to the saboteurs. He'd told them: 'Keep up the good work and I will provide the silver bullets.' Hywel

Hughes told me on the phone from his ranch: 'It was a phrase Lloyd George used in World War One to great effect. I said if they were to organise themselves they should be sure to have money behind them. I am proud that there are such worthy young men in Wales.'

That summer, for the first time, a hovercraft carried fare-paying passengers – between Wallasey and Rhyl. Small boys had to be cleared by a British United Airways marshal as they 'played chicken' with the 12-ton craft as it came on to the beach.

I broke the news in Bangor that their non-league soccer team was drawn to play mighty Naples in the European Cup Winners' Cup. In the *Herald* I wrote: 'To the east of Naples soars the volcanic cone of Vesuvius. To the south of Bangor rises the rugged peak of Snowdon. Both cities are crammed between mountains and the sea. Both have universities and 13th-century cathedrals. And there the resemblance ended – until now.' Mind you, Bangor didn't have the Mafia. Don't think so anyway, though there are a few drug barons these days.

Before an ecstatic crowd, Bangor did the impossible and won 2–0 at their ground, and that glorious night I slept on the floor of the Castle Hotel. The return match in Naples saw the Italians triumph 3–1. Under modern rules Bangor would have gone through under the away goals system. There was a play-off at Highbury, London, and the gallant Welsh part timers lost 2–1.

I had the page one lead with the story of a railway inquiry into a Boxing Night crash near Crewe which cost 18 lives. The driver of an express admitted with blinding honesty: 'I ignored a signal because I thought I had wasted enough time.'

Some stories, as one might say, you couldn't make up. One night Lord Snowdon popped into the 37-bed Bryn Seiont Hospital in Caernarfon to visit a patient who used to nurse him when he was a little boy living locally. So thrilled was Annie Jones to see him again she presented the hospital with specially made oak plaques – saying 'Tony Ward' and 'Snowdon Ward', and they were duly screwed to the entrance doors. There was a small ceremony and a picture appeared in the local paper. And that was how the 'hospital group committee' got to know – and ordered that the plaques be taken down.

'Wards must be named with the approval of the committee and can't be named after individual persons,' declared the hospital group secretary, severely. 'The plaques were put up without the authority of the committee and in direct contravention of a committee rule.'

Rules are rules, nothing changes... the word of the committee must be law. Particularly in Wales, the land of the committee.

The Queen and Prince Philip paid a royal visit to Caernarfon and Pwllheli. In Pwllheli the Queen visited Butlin's, the first by a monarch to a holiday camp, which happened to be at the site of HMS *Glendower* where Prince Philip had served during the war.

Weeds were removed, paint was applied and the disused railway station in Dinas, near Caernarfon, was reopened for the occasion so that they could travel by train to Pwllheli. The headline on my story read: 'Ghost station John says "No" to the Royals.' He was stationmaster at Groeslon and nominally in charge of the derelict platform in Dinas, but he had no intention of meeting royalty – because it was his 65th birthday that day and he was going to retire the day before. 'I was asked to officiate but it will be my 65th birthday on that day and I WILL retire,' he explained. 'I don't like fuss and ceremony and I would rather let someone else meet the Queen.'

One thing journalism has taught me is that it takes all sorts. In Manchester I met some of the fascinating characters of journalism.

A whisky drinking colleague was sent to Ireland for the Shannon air crash. He became 'tired and emotional', as *Private Eye* would say, fell from a balcony and was patched up by an

Irish chemist. When he returned to the office he looked... like he'd been patched up!

The night news editor would spend the early hours in the Press Club. On one bitter winter's early morning, the sound of a car being revved violently could be heard outside the office. It was Harry trying to move it. Thieves had removed the wheels, but Harry hadn't noticed.

One Christmas there was a train crash on the main line in Cheshire. That night reporters tried to get the local signalman to talk, but he refused. The time had come to withdraw from outside his home because it was obvious he was not going to cooperate. Along came an over-enthusiastic young man from the *Daily Telegraph* who wouldn't heed advice. An upper window opened – and the liquid contents of a chamber pot landed on his head. It was a story which improved with the telling in the newspaper pubs of Manchester.

Doing late duty one night there was a mini riot at a Sikh's bachelor party, involving 50 guests all named Singh. A knife was produced – though not used. That great character and wonderful writer Ian Skidmore had a page lead in the *Daily Mirror* with an intro which read: 'It was just one of those Singhs – but which one, police are asking today?'

During my five years in Manchester, Philip, Nigel and Alison were born. In those days dads did not attend births – thank goodness – but merely turned up at the bedside when it was all over.

I was getting a taste for returning to north Wales. So I decided to start as a one-man freelance, giving in my notice to the *Herald*. I knew the risk wasn't too great because each Saturday I had my Manchester shift on the *News of the World* to support me. It was a friendly environment and I worked under some great northern editors. They included Charlie Markus, Bill Taylor (who I believe narrowly missed being on HMS *Hood* for her final tragic voyage), and George McIntosh. I was getting the best of both worlds.

9

My own boss

IN NOVEMBER 1963, the month of Kennedy's assassination, I began self-employment. My first call was to reintroduce myself to the helicopter rescue crews at RAF Valley, the source of hundreds of stories subsequently. Now, after all those successful years, they've been partially privatised and after half a century we no longer get first-hand accounts from the crews. The work of the coastguard helicopters goes largely unreported, which is wrong.

My first story was 'RAF corporal saves climber', for which I was paid two pounds, twelve shillings and sixpence by the *Daily Mirror*, and two pounds, two shillings by the *Daily Mail*. Better was to come, with an eight-guinea payment for an exclusive for the *Sunday Mirror* – 'Undies factory in Holyhead town hall'. (A guinea was one pound and one shilling.)

That winter of 1963, one of the coldest on record, I stayed at my parents' home in Colwyn Bay, driving back to Manchester each Friday night and on the Saturday doing my *News of the World* stint. By the spring of 1964 it was evident that freelancing was going to be a success, so we bought a corner semi in Penrhyn Bay.

In the next few years Diane and Glyn were born. Both Glyn and Nigel were later to work for me at different times. Glyn is now my boss! Now, after first reporting and then producing for the BBC, HTV, and Granada, Nigel is a freelance series producer based in the USA, specialising in crime re-enactment and history shows. He reckons he's 'killed' well over 100 people in just about every conceivable way on television!

Alison was a physical education teacher for many years at Roedean, that posh girls' school in Brighton, but has now landed her dream job as head of PE at Benenden. Diane, with four children, has been a midwife at Glan Clwyd Hospital. Philip drives to Birkenhead daily for his IT job. He has had a work ethic from an early age (which I like to think he inherited from his father!) and a self-taught knowledge of computing.

From the start freelancing was a successful venture, mainly because I was on personal name terms with all the news editors, daily and Sunday. In those days there was intense competition, particularly for exclusives. North Wales had for years been covered only scantily.

I would drive many miles a week.

Unlike today, when data can be transmitted worldwide at the press of a computer key, in those days copy had to be dictated to copytakers, often lugubrious, short-tempered individuals – though there were some notable exceptions, particularly the women on the *Guardian*. But how off-putting it was to be asked, with a barely concealed sigh: 'Is there much more of this?' or 'Is that it, then?' Sometimes you heard him saying to his colleague: 'It's a load of bollocks.' Probably he was right!

Sometimes the copy had to be phoned to six or seven destinations. If a story changed in the meantime, it all had to be done again. Before many months had passed I began to know most phone boxes in north Wales. Shirley would help out, and as they grew older so would the children.

They were great days for newspapers, with titles vying for good stories. Being self-employed and relying on my own endeavours was a new and stimulating way of life. It was vital to buy a national insurance stamp each week and to take out sickness insurance, even though I never had to use it. I also invested in pension schemes, though Equitable Life was to become an unmitigated disaster. I still have their leaflet which boasts: 'You've chosen the best performing plan. With no hidden traps.' A barefaced lie when there were underlying problems.

There were good months and bad months, but the good were more common. In those days a story on BBC Wales was worth seven shillings and sixpence. An exclusive in the *Daily Mirror* made £7.

With the help of my solicitor friend, the late John Bellis (no relation), I won an important battle with the taxman who was unhappy about Shirley becoming a partner in the business. We went to an Inland Revenue tribunal and won hands down, John producing a long list of professions which had husband-and-wife partnerships, ranging from engineers to funeral directors. When I explained that Shirley often phoned copy and that this could be a lengthy process, the man from the Revenue found it difficult to understand. He was under the erroneous impression (probably from watching too many B movies) that copy was taken down in shorthand by women copytakers. Had that been so, life would have been so much easier.

In 1972 we moved to Old Budget Gate, a lovely detached house on the seafront in Rhos-on-Sea, so-named because a landowner had erected a tollgate outside to recoup the tax he had to pay when Lloyd George introduced old age pensions. We stayed there for 25 happy years.

Twice I was chairman of the North Wales Coast branch of the NUJ. But I left the union in the 1980s because it was becoming a far-left mouthpiece. I had always considered the duty of unions (and I had been vice-chairman of the branch in Manchester, the second largest outside London) was to look after the interests of their members, not to campaign to ban the bomb or be embroiled in some South American Marxist cause. Tragically, now, when more than ever journalists need protection, there is still a far-left bias. It has even supported Impress, the Press regulator beloved (and financed) by Max Mosley, and supported by Press-hating celebrities.

I joined the National Association of Press Agencies, comprising freelance journalists and photographers from throughout Britain (and also abroad) who meet periodically to consider common problems. Meetings in London, the Cotswolds, Birmingham and other centres have been worth attending – both socially and because of the tips and stories that are exchanged. Freelancers need a voice, because it is one of the few callings in which the customer, not the provider, decides the payment. In 2011 I was presented in London with NAPA's Lifetime Achievement Award.

Just as my late friend Jim Price of the *Daily Express* had prophesied jocularly, over the years my political leanings became more to the right as I got wiser. Working for myself and paying my taxes, I became upset by the freeloaders in our society, and still am. I see people in court who are paid by the state to stay at home and indulge in drink and drugs. Until this scandal – and that of political correctness, overdone health and safety and the compensation culture – is tackled, this nation will struggle. There is also the scandal of huge payments to officials of public bodies. One such person, in north Wales and already retired, gets an extra £70,000 on top of a big pension – for a part-time appointment.

Once I was asked if I was interested in becoming a Liberal parliamentary candidate for my local constituency. I still have the letter, but turned down the opportunity because politics and being a newsman wouldn't mix. There was integrity and my freedom to report to be considered.

I suppose my most productive years were in the 1980s and 1990s when I did hundreds of broadcasts for Radio Wales. At one stage I was up at 5 a.m. daily to get to the Point of Ayr colliery to watch workers being escorted past an angry picket line during the miners' strike. Once I had obtained the 'actuality' of shouts of 'scab' and other insults on the ancient Uher recording machine, and added a few words of my own, I would drive to the studio in Mold in time for the 7 a.m. bulletin. One morning, memorably, I was for some mysterious reason the source of the strikers' ire – and how my mischievous friend Jim relished it!

I recorded Arthur Scargill, hearing him, memorably, telling one meeting that he 'had it on the highest authority' that the lights would go out the following Wednesday. It never happened. My most vivid and saddest memory of the strike relates to one morning as the coach carrying the 'scabs' drove past the pickets. A striking miner, his face contorted with anger, screamed: 'I hope you all get cancer.' Seeing such hatred and loathing shook me.

Now, Point of Ayr is shut down, despite having some of the finest methane deposits in Britain. The 'oil from coal' experimental plant, on which millions was lavished, has gone too. It was all such a waste – in human, economic and industrial terms.

In the 1970s I also covered the firemen's strike. Like that of the miners and building workers, it was particularly bitter in north Wales. Some firemen who refused to walk out for reasons of conscience – and one from Rhyl in particular who had a breakdown in health because of the cruelty and abuse he suffered from his former workmates – were treated disgracefully by Clwyd County Council, which acted like an adjunct of the Fire Brigades Union (FBU). The council and unforgiving strikers were excoriated in a series of articles by Lynda Lee-Potter in the *Daily Mail* in 1978. The 'Rhyl seven' were the victims of trade unionism at its worst. One had protested: 'How could I strike when my sister had died in a fire?' Conscience made no difference; these men were ostracised, and were ignored when they turned to their employer for help. I was once, like my father, a proud trade unionist, but when I saw the behaviour of the FBU I was ashamed. But I've always had the greatest regard for fire fighters themselves and have enjoyed telling stories of their bravery.

I loved my radio work. I found it an easier and more pleasant medium than TV in which I was uncomfortable and self-conscious. I interviewed many famous people – Mrs Thatcher, Denis Healey, David Owen and Michael Foot to name just a few. What I did dislike, with my clumsy fingers, was cutting and threading recording tape. The journalists I worked with on radio were for the most part friendly and efficient. The boss, the late Gareth Bowen, father of the BBC's now Middle East editor Jeremy, told me I was a good radio journalist and I valued that encouragement.

Of course in broadcasting, as in newspapers, there were some mighty egos and we were reaching the stage where many journalists got senior jobs straight from university instead of through the ranks of weekly and evening papers. Some were adept at presenting and commenting on stories but they didn't have any experience of actually finding them. There were and still are many fine journalists working for the BBC. One has only to tune in to *Wales Today* on TV to see some brilliant new talent.

At the Bangor studios a security man in recent years joked that they no longer kept the door firmly locked to keep out Welsh-language protesters. 'We don't bother any longer,' he grinned – 'because they work here now.' These days, however, because of terrorist threats there is airport-type security.

When the *Wales on Sunday* paper was launched it caused the *Sunday Times* some initial worry, so it brought out a Welsh edition. I was asked to provide a story a week, which appeared with my byline. Suddenly, after six months, it all ended. Recently, however, it has reintroduced a Welsh edition, and it led the paper with our award-nominated story about the former north Wales NHS chief who went to London for cancer treatment because it was unavailable in Wales.

The *Daily Mirror*'s Welsh edition some years ago provided a goldmine for the four freelance news agencies in Wales. It was also a highly professional production. Then, as suddenly as it began, the edition finished. The *News of the World* produced a Welsh edition – which didn't appear much north of Cardiff. Welsh readers have never had a fair deal from the national dailies and Sundays, certainly not since Manchester closed down as a national newspaper centre.

As for the regionals, I worry about their constant staff reductions and cuts. It's sad that many courts and councils go uncovered in Britain. But handouts, from the police, MPs, members of the Welsh Assembly, councils, PR companies or anyone else, have become a godsend to much of the regional Press – because they're free. Often they appear as written and at length, rarely challenged. Stories which should merit a paragraph get almost a column. Alick Jeans and Glyn Rees must be spinning in their graves. In the old days these were regarded as 'puffs' and journalists told to investigate and if necessary challenge them. Nowadays, the longer the release is, the better. *Private Eye*'s 'Phil Space' lives on...

Good, proud journalists and cameramen on weeklies and dailies have lost their jobs, ostensibly because advertising has been filched by the internet giants. I must not be churlish, there are many aspects of modern newspapers, national and regional, which I admire. But not the cut-and-paste mentality...

10

All the news fit to print

WHEN I STARTED to freelance my friends in Manchester and London looked after me, but the work was hard. Some of it involved major inquiries for the *People*, a campaigning Sunday newspaper.

I did one major investigation to try and establish whether 'backhanders' were paid by undertakers to hospitals and nursing homes to get trade. 'It costs five guineas to be cremated in Colwyn Bay, only half as much as the fee in Wrexham,' I was told. Coffins were bought in bulk from a Preston firm described as 'the Rolls-Royce of coffin makers'.

Undertakers, unsurprisingly, denied giving tips to hospitals, police or hotels, though one admitted he was generous at Christmas to people who put business his way. Another, from Liverpool, spent £150 each Christmas on bottles of whisky for priests who had 'helped'. A mortuary attendant at a big Liverpool hospital was described as 'worth knowing'.

Another inquiry was into old folks' homes. And if there was one facility that Colwyn Bay and Llandudno didn't lack, and still doesn't, it was these. My brief was to visit these places and present my findings, as if they were hotels.

Frequently I was asked to investigate what was on offer for holidaymakers at our resorts. One night I stayed at a Llandudno hotel on behalf of the *Sunday Express*. I presented my findings and was critical that they'd neglected to provide enough towels. Such a fuss this minor criticism produced, and the town's hoteliers couldn't have been more agitated had I found a rat under the bed.

I wrote a story in the *News of the World* entitled '*Peyton Place* report shocks Welsh valley'. It was an archetypal story for the *NoW* – a report written by a sociologist from Manchester University about sexual life in a Merionethshire parish embracing Llanfrothen, Rhyd and Croesor.

My introduction read: 'In pub and country village the talk in a quiet, beautiful Welsh valley is of the Emmett Report – and what it says about the locals. For the report speaks of the high illegitimacy rate; forced marriages; women known as 'good things'; and a double set of values which reconciles chapel-going with loose living.'

Some locals attacked the report but others, including a Cambridge MA turned hill farmer, thought the authoress had a point.

The following week the news editor, George McIntosh, phoned me. 'Derek, we've had a complaint,' he said. (Those are always dreaded words.) 'A lady in Croesor wants to know why you didn't call to see her. She's upset at being left out…'

You never know how people will react. There was an industrial tribunal case in which a hospital's decision to fire a porter because of his lack of personal hygiene was upheld. Some years later I was stopped by a man on the street in Bangor. 'Do I know you?' I asked him. 'Don't you remember – I'm "Mr Smelly",' he grinned, proud of the name with which he'd been endowed.

In pre-computer days I wrote my stories in thick exercise books, which I have preserved to this day. If a family member were to phone the story it would have been typed on my trusty Remington, which I have also kept for old times' sake.

In July 1966 the secretary of the National Federation of Sub-Postmasters declared at their Llandudno conference that hundreds of women working in sub-post offices were 'genuinely' frightened of being attacked. There had been three deaths in a little more than a year and it was suggested that bulletproof glass and 'spray guns' at the counter could be the answer. It was decided to ask the Postmaster General, Mr Wedgwood Benn, to discuss improving security. Half a century later sub-postmasters are still vulnerable to attack. The only thing that's changed is that often the attackers are drug-crazed and many offices have now closed.

At another conference, the National Association of Colliery Overmen, Deputies and Shotfirers – better known as NACODS – grumbled that the miners they bossed were getting more money than them. It was a familiar situation to the newspaper industry, where the electricians, the printers and the wrappers-up were making small fortunes sometimes under made-up names to fool the taxman and by always threatening to strike, or by 'accidentally' breaking the reel of newsprint. Yet the journalists, because of their lack of clout, had to endure low wages. Those NACODS delegates were assured by the government that there was 'a big future' in their industry. Hmm...

I provided material for comment pieces in the Sunday papers, usually the *News of the World* and for John Junor's famous column in the *Sunday Express*. In the *News of the World* I castigated the council at my home town of Colwyn Bay. 'Councillors at some of our resorts seem to have the odd notion that visitors should pay through the nose to enjoy those sea breezes,' I wrote. 'No one, it appears, should be allowed to return home without having made a substantial contribution to local funds.'

The council had cordoned off a grass verge on the promenade to make it into a picnic spot where visitors could park their cars and enjoy a picnic. The cost was five shillings – a fair sum in those days – and the idea was to 'discourage' families from cluttering the prom itself with folding chairs, portable stoves and other picnic paraphernalia. I pointed out it could have the opposite effect – by discouraging families from stopping in Colwyn Bay. Anyway, the idea was soon abandoned. Whether my stricture played any part, I don't know.

There was embarrassment one Saturday night when I turned up in Manchester for my shift on the *News of the World*. There was a call for me – from John Junor, editor-in-chief of the *Sunday Express* and one of the giants of British journalism. But I was able to assure my colleagues that what I had written for him was not the sort of material which would interest the *NoW*. Happy days...

It's funny how some stories stick in your mind. There was an eminent surgeon at the Caernarfon and Anglesey General Hospital in Bangor who had a fixation about cross-infection. He realised the dangers and it makes you wonder that, if he'd been heeded and there were more like him today, MRSA and C. diff might not be the deadly problems that they have become.

Mr Skyrme Rees made a succession of allegations, bringing up example after example of bad practice. Getting nowhere, he decided to involve the newspapers. With my colleague Jim Price of the *Daily Express*, I would turn up at the surgeon's home overlooking the Menai Strait and he would regale us with the latest horrors. The hospital board would issue reassuring but unconvincing rebuttals and assurances. Eventually, after a deluge of stories, the committee announced it would in future refrain from issuing any statements of rebuttal.

Thus I was able to break the final story without even having to approach them. I can still see it, the back page lead of the *Daily Sketch*. Skyrme Rees described how he had been in the middle of an operation when a manhole cover was raised in the theatre. A workman popped his head through, then said 'So sorry' before putting down the lid and disappearing. Talk about cross-infection!

For the management this was the last straw. A deal was made with Skyrme Rees, complete with gagging clause to prevent him, presumably, from revealing any more unpalatable truths, and he disappeared to Australia. I believe he became one of that country's most eminent surgeons. Strange, isn't it, how officialdom goes into denial so often when faced with the truth? And how good men are lost.

One of the joys of journalism is in discovering the bizarre and laughable things that go on. Like in Llanfyllin, near Oswestry, familiar to me because I spent childhood holidays on a farm nearby. It had a rural district council and also an urban council – and shared a clerk. So, frequently the clerk would write and sign letters to himself in an official capacity. As Richard Littlejohn would say, you couldn't make it up!

11

Amazing inquests

ONE BALMY JULY evening we sat outside one of the loveliest pubs in Wales, the George III in Penmaenpool near Dolgellau, overlooking the River Mawddach. As we quenched our thirsts my friend Bernard Howard of the *Daily Herald* said: 'We shouldn't really be doing this, should we?'

For beneath us, as the sun went down, was one of the saddest sights of my career. Every so often a shout would go up, boatmen would arrive, remove a body from the water, wrap it in a bodybag and it would be driven away. Fifteen died in the Mawddach estuary disaster, after which the rules relating to pleasure craft and their licensing were tightened, as they always are (until the next time) when such events shock the nation.

It was the worst disaster I had ever reported on. Families who had paid for a trip in the sun from Barmouth were spilled into the water when the pleasure boat touched a stanchion of the wooden Penmaenpool toll bridge and overturned. Men, women and children drowned, including a family of four. Others were saved by acts of bravery, including that of the landlord of the George III, John Hall, his barman and chef on that hot day in July 1966.

Four of the victims were children. The trip cost five shillings a head and there were 39 on the boat (there should have been no more than 35) with an experienced helmsman who had served as a brave and trusted lifeboatman in Barmouth. The boat, the *Prince of Wales*, was later burned – a symbolic and fitting end.

Weeks later the inquest began at 10 a.m. and ended after midnight, it being coroner Harry Evans Jones' wish that it should be completed in one sitting. We were dashing out of the courtroom in Dolgellau throughout the evening to give 'takes' on the evidence, then a final piece in the early hours. I have never been to any judicial event that lasted so long into the night. Whatever rules were broken, a strong tide, complacency and bad luck had contributed to the tragedy.

Whenever I pass the wooden bridge in Penmaenpool, my mind goes back to that sunny day. A Board of Trade inquiry blamed negligent handling and the absence of a crewman. In 2016 I attended a ceremony to mark the 50th anniversary – and shamefully not a line appeared in the national Press.

An inquest in Denbigh in 1991, conducted by that pleasant and thorough coroner Bryan Lewis, sounded like the plot from a cheap paperback. Given home leave from an open prison, 45-year-old 'lifer' Christopher Griffin was a kidnapper and sex offender. He killed himself with fumes inside a hire car on a lonely track in Llanelidan, near Ruthin – just three miles from where, in 1978, he'd trapped a Canadian woman tourist whom he'd kidnapped, gagged, cut away her clothing with a knife and whipped her. He'd also committed similar crimes against three female hitch-hikers.

Griffin had got the hire car by posing as a probation officer. In it was found an extract from an American crime novel he'd been reading in prison called *Perfect Victim*, which included a story about a woman being held for years in a coffin-style box. A chilling inquest...

I've been to hundreds of them, often feeling like a spectator to tragedy. The unlucky victims, the unwary, the careless, I've heard about them all. Tragedies like the one when a group of boys from a private school in London, on Snowdon at Easter, slid on their bottoms for fun on the compacted snow and ice – and plunged hundreds of feet to their deaths.

Most coroners I've found are caring and sensitive. Sometimes, as a reporter, I still feel like an interloper when families relate their tragic stories. The only happy inquests are those on treasure-trove.

For many hit by tragedy the doubt must arise: is there a loving God, as we've been taught? I know I felt the same when we lost our grandchild Charlotte when only three – a victim of not only Down's Syndrome but leukaemia.

However, a light of hope can shine even at appalling times. One was provided by my friend Bill Richardson, an artist who lovingly painted lifelike portraits of 116 of the child victims of the Aberfan tragedy, copying photographs provided by bereaved parents. He was the guest of George Thomas, the Secretary of State for Wales, who thanked him personally. Bill also worked for ten months on a 9ft by 5ft canvas depicting Christ receiving some of the children.

Sometimes a sixth sense seems to spot an impending tragedy. Such was the case when two men set off from Deganwy in 1974 intending to reach Australia aboard their 38ft sloop – with a concrete hull. Within a week it had been found wrecked on the rocks in Cornwall, and there was no sign of the two sailors. Vivien Pickering, 26, of Abergele had given up his job as a policeman intending to join the pair but had a change of mind three days before the send-off. 'I had a premonition she wouldn't even reach Cadiz and I just wasn't prepared to risk my life,' he explained.

Of the hundreds of inquests I've attended one stands out in particular. It was in Bangor in June 1972. With my colleagues Jim Price and Gerald Williams of the *Daily Post*, I was there to cover the story of a Manchester estate agent who drowned when driving his speedboat in ever decreasing circles in the Conwy estuary.

Coroner John Pritchard Jones (whose son Dewi has succeeded him) also held an inquest into the death of a sub -postmistress from the Conwy Valley, Gwen Parry Jones, a widow of 48 who died from alcohol poisoning. There was nothing out of the ordinary about the case – until a man who claimed to be her friend gave evidence.

I'd been out of court and had just returned after he'd taken the oath to begin his testimony. His name was Norman Scott and his evidence was uncontroversial – until the coroner asked about his background.

He announced that he'd lived with Jeremy Thorpe, the then leader of the Liberal Party, for six years, in a relationship, and that Mr Thorpe had documents which belonged to him. 'Are you his agent?' queried the puzzled coroner. 'No, I live with him,' said Scott, who went on to describe a dispute with the Liberal leader about payment of his National Insurance stamp.

I still have the note of the most sensational story I ever wrote – and which never appeared.

Jim, Gerald (a master of shorthand) and I excitedly debated what to do. We checked our notes and decided we had to consult news desks. For Jim and Gerald that was no problem, they only had to deal with one. I had to tell the news desks of every national paper. I was late contacting the *Telegraph*, so they rang me instead after the story had passed through the Fleet Street rumour factory like a whirlwind.

Instructions from each was identical: 'A full memo, please, with every word he said.' That night I believe that Emlyn Hooson, the QC and prominent member of the Liberal Party, headed an emergency meeting in the Commons. This time it was NOT 'publish and be damned' – the story was not carried by a single newspaper. Apparently the official Liberal Party line used to persuade editors was that Scott was mentally deranged – a lie. This was one of the most amazing stories any of us had ever covered. And it was astonishing that it didn't see the light of day.

The following afternoon I was sitting at my desk in Penrhyn Bay when the phone rang. 'Mr Bellis?' 'Yes.' 'This is Jeremy Thorpe.' At first I thought it a leg-pull, then realised it was the authentic voice of the leader of the Liberal Party. 'My faith in the British Press has been restored,' he declared. I didn't know whether to feel proud or ashamed. Then he said: 'Next time you are in London you must have dinner with me.' It's a dinner date I never kept.

Later, of course, the whole story unravelled and Thorpe was cleared in a sensational conspiracy to murder trial. Should the newspapers have published the story, safe to do because what is said at inquests is privileged and so without any risk of defamation proceedings? I think the claim – and rebuttal – should have been carried. Of one thing I'm certain. Today that story would have been on EVERY front page. Now, of course, the whole saga has been reproduced in a wonderful TV serial.

There is one inquest that haunts me, even today. It was of a 25-year-old Penmaenmawr woman who died in Risley Remand Centre six days after being refused bail (wrongly in my view) by magistrates in Llandudno. She was charged with cannabis offences but was suffering from Hodgkin's Disease and psychiatric problems. 'Sad and dispirited', she had died in the night, having been unable to summon help to her cell when she became ill. I went to the inquest in Warrington and I thought the tragedy was glossed over. Sending that tortured soul to prison was the worst possible option, yet it was chosen. She didn't deserve to die, locked in a cell unable to get help.

Many inquests are heartbreaking. Like that of a toddler of 18 months who died of thirst in a first-floor flat in the town centre of Rhyl, his drug-taking parents dead nearby. Syringes and drugs were scattered around the room – as were unopened Christmas toys. It was a tragedy which had a major effect on the police officers unfortunate enough to have been involved. Canon Herbert Lloyd, that wonderful vicar, summed it up: 'Living in the centre of a town can be very impersonal and sometimes you hardly know your neighbours. It can be so different from living within a community, like you see on *Coronation Street*. Many of these flats are occupied by people who are not local, and some of them have no jobs. I can only hope that something good comes out of this tragedy – a little more concern about neighbourliness.'

Tragedy, too, befell solicitor Paul McGowran, whom I interviewed for radio and wrote about in the national papers when he left Prestatyn in 1991 on a round-the-world motorcycle trip to raise money for cancer charities. He had many adventures, met the Dalai Lama, married a Thai bride, Chutima, then was killed as they rode through Indonesia. She'd been riding separately ahead of him, and had to swerve to avoid a speeding tourist bus on the wrong side of the road – which killed her husband.

They'd ridden together through South Korea, China, Tibet, Vietnam and Cambodia and also visited Japan. She told the inquest in Prestatyn that her husband was a meticulous and careful rider. In their few years together they had seen more of the world than most people see in a lifetime, only for a cruel twist of fate to end their life together. His sponsored ride raised £50,000 to fight cancer. At the inquest in 1998 his half-brother Terence, a solicitor from Solihull, said with a smile: 'I don't think a nine-to-five existence suited Paul.'

One of the strangest inquests, in 1988, was on 42-year-old Philip March who starved himself to death deliberately in a remote part of Gwydyr Forest. He'd been dead nearly 18 months when his body was discovered in a sleeping bag in a tent in dense undergrowth – with a copy of the *Radio Times* open on 28 June 1986. Inside the tent were a radio, Bible, cassettes and religious books and he was wearing a crucifix and chain. There was no food but water had been gathered by using a groundsheet to funnel it into a mess tin. The coroner decided that because of his religious beliefs Mr March had decided to kill himself by starvation and not some other method.

Not far away in 1998 the charred body of 25-year-old Georgio Castellera was found in a burned-out car at a remote spot off the A5 near the Swallow Falls in Betws-y-Coed. He was a London car salesman and coroner John Hughes, recording at open verdict, said there was 'a lack of evidence in crucial areas'. Ethiopian-born Rita Hunt of London offered a £50,000 reward to anyone who could solve the mystery, believing her son had been the victim of the perfect murder. She had handed to the police a list of suspects whom she believed could have killed her 6' 6" son, a keen casino gambler. 'Somebody did this terrible thing to my son,' she declared, 'he would not even think to kill himself.' He'd been alive when the car exploded but according to a pathologist it was impossible to say whether he was conscious.

12

The Investiture

JULY 1ST, 1969, was the day thousands in Wales will never forget. The 'Arwisgo' (Investiture) of Prince Charles as Prince of Wales in the 13th-century castle in Caernarfon. It was the culmination of months of preparation, protests, bombs and intense political debate.

For six weeks Prince Charles had been at University College of Wales, Aberystwyth, taking what was described as 'a crash course in Welshness'. Most weekends I would be sent by the *Sunday Mirror* on a 180-mile round trip to cover his activities. One weekend he travelled to Caernarfon for a look around the castle and the special dais. American tourists who had a few hours earlier disembarked from a cruise ship in Llandudno couldn't believe their luck. 'Gee, doesn't he look great – this has made our trip,' they swooned.

A month before the Investiture I had been at the Urdd (Welsh League of Youth) annual Eisteddfod in Aberystwyth when the Prince spoke Welsh in public for the first time. I still have my accounts of the event from the *Sunday Mirror* and the *Guardian*, describing how the 20 year old achieved a Saturday night triumph in what must have been a great ordeal. He had to endure the boorish hostility of a hundred protesters who took out banners and shouted slogans before walking out.

My account in the *Guardian* concluded: 'As the thousands left the Eisteddfod, there was a great deal of bitterness about the demonstration – though the fact that only one hundred out of 5,000 people had taken part was quoted as a major consolation and as evidence of the weakness of the zealots. The feeling was expressed that now the extremists had gone too far. "Chwarae teg" (fair play) has always been a favourite expression in Wales.'

That has been one of the pleasures of freelancing, writing late one night (very much against the clock) for a Sunday tabloid, the next day finding a different mindset to compose for the *Guardian* or the *Times*.

The Investiture organiser, the Duke of Norfolk (the premier duke in the peerage), visited the castle a few weeks before to take stock. Rain was pouring and he was asked what would happen if it were the same on the great day. 'People will get wet,' he replied tartly, a remark which some thought a typical and humorous stiff-upper-lip reply to be expected from the aristocracy. He didn't endear himself to TV and Press photographers especially invited by the Welsh Office. The scribes and cameramen claimed the Duke had demanded: 'How long are this lot going to be here? Get them out.' And with that the heavy doors of the castle were slammed in their faces.

For some it was seen as an event, promoted by Harold Wilson's Labour Government, to marginalise the rapidly emerging Plaid Cymru and organisations such as the Welsh Language Society who were in the midst of their campaign to get bilingual road signs – having gone on massive expeditions to cover English signs with green paint.

To an extent Wales was polarised. But it was those who were against the Investiture who naturally were the more noisy and attracted the media attention. Surprisingly, the Archdruid-elect, the Rev. Gwilym Tilsley, was concerned that Wales was missing out in the souvenirs market. 'All sorts of English firms seem to be cashing in,' he pointed out. 'It seems a shame that we in Wales are making all this fuss about the Investiture, yet the people reaping the real profit will be firms in England.'

The Wales Tourist Board was busy explaining that it was quite unnecessary to pay £100 for a week's furnished accommodation to coincide with the royal event, because a family of five could get a quite reasonable cottage for twenty guineas.

Dafydd Iwan, 25, the folk-singing leader of the Welsh Language Society, composed a satirical song entitled 'Carlo' which he sung to his guitar accompaniment. It leapt up to No. 1 in the Welsh charts. The opening lyrics, translated, were: 'I've got a friend who lives in Buckingham Palace, Carlo Windsor is his name.' A chorus included the words: 'Carlo's playing polo today, Carlo's playing polo with Daddy.' Hardly Tim Rice standard, yet thousands found the lyrics amusing.

The song was played over loudspeakers at an anti-Investiture rally on St David's Day in Caernarfon attended by 4,000 people. 'The last true Prince of Wales died in 1282,' declared Mr Iwan. 'The Investiture is a public declaration of the subjugation of Wales to the English crown... a political gimmick instituted in 1911 by Lloyd George, and the present regime is using Prince Charles as a pawn for its own political reasons. The show of military strength at the ceremony is the product of an imperialistic power and is alien to the spirit of Wales.'

Ifor Bowen Griffith, the mayor of Caernarfon, had a different view. He said Prince Charles spoke more good sense in 20 minutes than his opponents did in a year. For his pains he was accused by his opponents of kowtowing to the Establishment. My friend Reg Jones of the *Mirror* remembers a wonderful exchange between the mayor and the Prince. 'I.B. Griffith,' said the mayor, proffering his hand. 'I be Charles,' laughed the Prince, grasping it.

The BBC came in for criticism for an item on their *24 Hours* TV programme in which a souvenir Investiture mug was smashed. Councillor Mrs Megan Bonner Pritchard said: 'Feelings in the town are running high because the broadcast painted the worst possible picture. Friends of mine in London have told me they are absolutely shocked.' Accusing both the BBC and ITV of favouring the views of a minority, she protested: 'At least 80 per cent of the people of Caernarfon are for the Investiture.'

John Eilian Jones, a Tory, bard and editor of the *Caernarfon and Denbigh Herald*, said in an editorial: 'The people of Caernarfon and indeed of all north Wales are unhappy at the calculated anti-Investiture tone of nearly all BBC and ITV broadcasts from Caernarfon.'

A few days before the Investiture a great team had arrived in the town from the *Express*, reporters and cameramen from both Manchester and Fleet Street. They thought, wrongly, that when their hotel proprietor went to bed they had a deal with him to keep the bar open while they refreshed the till. In the early hours, hearing the commotion, he came downstairs and exploded with anger. A police inspector was called and the journos, like naughty schoolboys, packed their suitcases and traipsed through Caernarfon pre-dawn begging for a bed for the night. It was a wrong call by the owner. Had he accommodated his guests he could have made a fortune – they were probably the thirstiest crew he had ever encountered.

Late on the eve of the Investiture two men, Alwyn Jones, 22, and George Taylor, 37, were killed when a bomb they were carrying exploded close to a government building in Abergele, 35 miles from Caernarfon. The two council workers had just left a pub and to this day there's controversy about whether their target had been the building, or the main north Wales coast railway line half a mile away where the royal train was due to pass.

We'll never know, though at the inquest in Abergele that punctilious coroner, E. Talog Davies, said the indications were that they intended the explosion to take place where it did – outside the Ministry of Social Security offices. 'It seemed they had no intention of hurting anyone, though there was always the possibility that someone could have been in the vicinity,' he observed.

Significantly, he said: 'Someone who knew more about explosives than they did gave either Jones or Taylor, or both, a substantial quantity of high explosive. You may well feel,' he told the jury, 'that a very grave responsibility for the deaths lies upon such a person.' For many years there was a memorial march through Abergele each July, and at one stage some of the participants were in paramilitary uniforms. One or two, I felt, may have marched because of pangs of conscience.

In 1994 seven men went a step too far when they turned up in black berets, sunglasses and white shirts proclaiming 'Meibion Glyndŵr'. They got conditional discharges after a summons under the 1936 Public Order Act was brought, accusing them of wearing uniforms 'signifying an association with a political organisation or with the promotion of a political object'. Magistrates, in forgiving mood, allowed them to retain their clothing – apart from the badges.

The day of the Investiture arrived. There had been a threat that hundreds would swoop on Caernarfon to show their displeasure at the 'treachery'. There were 2,200 extra police drafted in to Caernarfon. The cost to Gwynedd Police Authority for the officers' food, accommodation and transport was £25,000.

Commander Jock Wilson of Scotland Yard was put in charge of security, operating from Shrewsbury, which many took as an insult to the local police. It was true that the Home Office didn't entirely trust Welsh police, which also explained why some of the most sensitive and armed work on the great day was performed by officers from across the border.

I was given a ticket for the Investiture and was in the ramparts with a bird's-eye view of the panoply and the ritual. Next to me was Det. Sgt. Elfyn Williams, then with the Special Branch. He'd been a friend for many years and later became a councillor and a member of the North Wales Police Authority. There was nervousness, compounded half an hour before the royal party was due to parade through the streets by the sound of an explosion. A bomb had gone off, harmlessly, close to the home of the Chief Constable, Lieutenant-Colonel William Jones-Williams.

In the event, the ceremony passed off peacefully, though a few days later ten-year-old holidaymaker Ian Cox lost his right foot when a bomb which had been planted 100 yards from the royal route exploded. It was a tragedy which I thought, and still do, was too quickly forgotten and minimised.

On the whole the Prince got a great welcome in Wales. By some he was derided, but generally he was greeted with warmth. After all, he was just 20.

Immediately after the ceremony I was asked by the *Express* to get the impressions of the teenage daughter of Arthur Rowlands, a very brave policeman blinded in the course of duty when he was shot on a river bank near Machynlleth. I still have the paper today, and the page one story. It read: 'In row 10 behind the dais sat Carol Rowlands, pupil at Caernarvon Grammar School [Caernarfon was still spelled with a 'v' in those days].

'She is the 18-year-old daughter of Mr Arthur Rowlands, former policeman awarded the George Medal after being blinded by a gunman. Carol was there as a representative of Caernarvonshire youth.'

Daily Express Investiture front page, 1969

Afterwards she said: 'All Wales should be proud of the Prince today. He was wonderful and his speech in Welsh was also wonderful.

'I could tell he was nervous but he overcame it. His pronunciation was very good...'

Two funny incidents stay in my mind. With more policemen in Caernarfon than in its entire history, one man chose to 'flash' in the crowded square. His was one of the few arrests.

A few hours after the Investiture a special court was held in Caernarfon at which nine people appeared, most of them for what today would be called public order offences, generally being fined £5.

Two 18-year-old lads admitted flicking an offensive V-sign as the royal carriages went by. One had told police if people were allowed to go there to express their approval, 'then we should be allowed to go to express our disapproval'. A 16-year-old boy was accused of throwing a banana skin under the feet of Household Cavalry horses and was dealt with at the juvenile court, no doubt also fined. And the flasher? Fined £10.

After the Investiture 4,400 chairs on which guests had sat, designed in part by Lord Snowdon, were put on sale at £12 each by the Ministry of Works – I have one myself which has worn well. Castle guests were given first choice and bought 2,150. They were a sell-out and fetched £50,000.

The chairs were made in Wales at Remploy factories, the frames of beech stained in vermillion, and the seat and back of pre-formed plywood.

Among guests who paid £12 were the Prime Minister Harold Wilson, Earl Mountbatten, Senator Hubert Humphrey of the USA (who had links with Wales) and Tricia Nixon, daughter of the president. Others were Edward Heath, Selwyn Lloyd, and John Silkin who was Minister of Public Buildings and Works.

Chairs were also ordered by VIPs, including ambassadors

from all over the world. There are so many of them their worth is still modest.

It was only 40 years after the event that retired Det. Sgt. Elfyn Williams, who recently died, revealed his secret. Like some others in the castle he carried a revolver. The snag was he wasn't issued with a holster. So he kept it in his briefcase. A good job there wasn't a shoot-out!

When Det. Chief Supt. Gwynne Owen, a good friend, retired in 1988 he recalled his time in charge of Special Branch between 1967 and 1972, which involved security arrangements for the Investiture. 'Looking back it is the enormity of the event, the biggest in north Wales since 1911, which stays in the memory,' he told me. 'Threats had been made against several personalities and I must say there was a feeling of relief when it was all over.'

The army had put up a Bailey bridge across the River Seiont in Caernarfon to enable Investiture guests to park their cars in fields across the river. It was so popular that afterwards locals sent a 'Save our Bridge' petition to Harold Wilson, but to no avail. The council had even offered to pay rent of £174 a week to the army.

Controversy continued after the Investiture. The official newspaper of Plaid Cymru complained about 'heavy-handed police' who dealt with demonstrators when Prince Charles visited the National Eisteddfod in Flint. 'Police officers piled in with the zest of a New Zealand pack,' it protested. 'We ask for police authorities in Wales to use a good deal more common sense than of late and that some of our tempestuous brethren in blue should play it a little more cool.'

I shook hands with the Prince when he visited a gold mine in a forest near Dolgellau. I've always been impressed by his sincerity. In June 2009 he presented my wife Shirley with an MBE for her voluntary work. There were 107 recipients that day at Buckingham Palace and when he chatted with every one of them he showed genuine interest in their stories. He's a good man. In these days of dodgy politicians and second-rate public servants, the royal family is an important constant.

Of course, politicians themselves were to blame for some of the anti-Englishness at the time of the Investiture. And when the history of Wales is written, Tryweryn will stand as the greatest modern crime committed against this nation. This beautiful valley near Bala was flooded in 1965 so that a reservoir could be created to quench the thirst of Liverpool. The villagers of Capel Celyn lost their homes and their land.

I was in Liverpool when the council – I believe it was Labour controlled – refused to meet a delegation from north Wales.

The official opening, with appalling insensitivity, took the form of a splendid lunch in a marquee beside the new dam. It was raining and protesters suddenly ran down the hillside. As the guests filed into the marquee for their lunch, they had to run the gauntlet of hundreds of angry Welsh men and women, many wielding umbrellas. A shamefaced local vicar was among the guests. 'What will God say about this?' demanded an outraged woman protester. The Chief Constable of Liverpool suffered the indignity of his car aerial being twisted. Forty years later the city of Liverpool proffered an official apology. Too late.

In Wales itself officialdom added fuel to the nationalistic fires. In Flint, magistrates imposed a charge of three guineas (a guinea was worth 21 shillings) on a 19-year-old student so he could have an interpreter to enable the case to be heard in Welsh. The student was fined £10 for pulling down a Union flag during the National Eisteddfod.

After the case had been reported in the local paper the three-guinea charge was cancelled. And the magistrates' clerk admitted in a letter: 'I confirm that a rule under the Welsh Courts (Oath and Interpreters) Rules 1943 says that no party to any proceedings conducted in Welsh shall be liable to pay any costs of the interpreter.'

Sometimes Prince Charles was let down by politicians and civil servants, with his special Welsh Countryside Committee of 31 (yes 31!) being packed with aristocracy, professors and county bigwigs, without a single trade unionist, housewife (apart from Lady Anglesey) or member of the Ramblers or Youth Hostels Association.

Later, the TUC in Wales attacked the composition of this royal committee, which an official spokesman declared had been chosen by 'the usual methods'. Too true!

Tom Jones, the north Wales trade unionist, Spanish Civil War hero and vice-chairman of the Welsh Economic Council, said: 'We want the ordinary people to be represented as well as the aristocrats and specialists.' To which the official spokesman retorted, typically and as if in justification: 'There is no TUC person on the English committee, either.'

When a public inquiry opened in Holyhead into a plan to build the £80 million aluminium smelter (unfortunately closed in the autumn of 2009), the Ministry of Housing, Communities and Local Government inspector decreed that anyone wishing to give evidence in Welsh could do so but that 'the recognised procedure' was that they paid their own costs. For the campaign being waged by language activists, such stupidity came as manna from heaven.

A quarter of a century after the Investiture, Prince Charles returned to Caernarfon Castle where there were 1,200 invited guests at a garden party to mark the occasion and thousands more lining the streets. This confounded the critics who claimed that it would be a washout, even if more than half the members of Caernarfon town council boycotted it.

Charles was always a fan of *The Goon Show*, and among the stars to greet him in the castle was the wonderful Sir Harry Secombe. 'Twenty-five years ago, Your Royal Highness stepped on this plinth, now known as the plinth of Wales,' he joked.

During the Investiture period we learned from the highest authority that journalists' phones were being bugged by police. There was nothing we could do about it – except leave rude messages for Jones-Williams, the Chief Constable, at the end of conversations!

With hindsight, the Investiture was more Gilbert and Sullivan than modern Britain. 'I Charles, do become your liege man of life and limb and of earthly worship...'

Somehow, I don't think this costly and controversial event will ever be repeated – certainly not at Caernarfon Castle.

13

Some violent campaigns

TOWARDS THE END of 1968 one of Wales's most famous trials took place at Caernarfon Assizes. In the dock was 35-year-old Owen Williams, a farmer from Pistyll, near Nefyn, who was accused of possessing gelignite.

Owen Williams was a dashing dark-haired figure who drove a smart red Volvo sports car and today is a Gwynedd county councillor, an outspoken member of Llais Gwynedd, a party set up to oppose plans by the majority Plaid Cymru group to close some rural schools.

During his evidence he denied having suggested a 'takeover' of Caernarfon Castle three days before the Investiture, or that he had heard anyone else saying as much. He was defended by the heavyweight – in every sense – QC, Andrew Rankin of Liverpool, who had made his name in a 'body in the cupboard' trial involving an acquitted Rhyl landlady.

Owen Williams described himself as vice-president of the non-violent National Patriotic Front but had never belonged to the Free Wales Army. He had jumped bail and spent six months in Ireland 'preparing his defence'.

Mr Justice Crichton, who handled the trial immaculately, reminded the jury: 'He is not in the dock for holding extreme Welsh nationalist views.'

When he was cleared after four days there was cheering and applause from 200 people who had crowded into the public gallery and outside.

At a triumphant Press conference in the Royal Hotel, Owen

Williams sported a yellow and red striped badge of the National Patriotic Front given to him by a supporter.

He said: 'It was a fair trial and it's wonderful to be free. I must have time to think about my political future; right now I can't say what it will be.

'I went to Ireland because I did not think my defence was ready. It was my plan to return after six months because I thought by then the guilty person would have come forward or otherwise it would give me time to arrange my defence adequately.

'The Patriotic Front wants Wales to be a republic, unlike Plaid Cymru which is for dominion status. I'm sure that self-government for Wales will soon be here.' Sentiments that 40 years later were at least half-true.

When he was in County Cork he'd planted potatoes and at one time lived in a tent. But on his arrest when he returned to Britain, he'd been subject to 'train robber style security'.

When he was moved from Risley Remand Centre to Bristol Prison, he was accompanied by eight prison officers, and handcuffed to two of them, with police cars in front and behind the van. 'I was told the reason I was not accommodated at a Welsh prison was because they were afraid of riots there,' he said.

At the Caernarfon court, he said, eight prison officers looked after him in the cells – four of whom watched him shave each morning. 'Though I knew I was innocent, the last ten months have been a great strain. Some of the things which have happened make me very angry but I do not bear grudges.'

Within a few days the charismatic nationalist – known to some fond admirers as 'the gallant Owen' – was in less intimidating surroundings, speaking to university students in Bangor.

I called at Owen Williams' farm on the afternoon before the Investiture, but he was not there. His mother pointed to Special Branch officers watching us through binoculars from across the valley. She told me how sometimes she would, for fun, peer back at THEM through binoculars. Likeable Owen – now known as Owain – never hurt anyone, and that rebellious streak remains.

In 1970 I was in Mold for the trial of Sgt. John Jenkins, 37, of the Royal Army Dental Corps, who described himself as director general of MAC – Mudiad Amddiffyn Cymru, the Free Wales Army, when he got ten years for his part in the Welsh bombing campaign. His friend Frederick Ernest Alders got six years. They were told by Mr Justice Thompson that Wales would expect them to be punished 'both for your own misdeeds and to discourage any others who may be disposed to imitate you'.

It was a trial which at times was more like a work of fiction: of a cloak-and-dagger interview given to two hooded journalists in Chester, my friend Harold Pendlebury of the *Daily Mail* and freelance Ian Skidmore; of explosives hidden in an army camp; and a claim that Jenkins's fanaticism had been kindled by the tragedy of Aberfan, the village near where he was brought up.

Jenkins had once said he expected 20 years if he was caught, so was probably relieved at the outcome. Strangely, two years later in the *Welsh Nation*, the official journal of Plaid Cymru, there were details of a Christmas fast for five jailed Welshmen – one of them Jenkins – behind bars 'for Wales and its language'. In fairness, the journal explained that this 'did not necessarily imply endorsement'. I should hope not!

Looking back, the legal line-up in that trial is fascinating, a triumvirate from the elite in Welsh judicial life. Prosecuting was Tasker Watkins QC, who won a VC when fighting with the Welch Regiment in the Second World War, and was later president of the Welsh Rugby Union, to whom a statue has been unveiled.

Defending Jenkins was Peter Thomas, the solicitor's son and QC from the Conwy Valley, shot down and a POW when in the RAF, and later to become Secretary of State for Wales and chairman of the Tory Party. While a POW he'd arranged an eisteddfod for his Welsh comrades. He said Jenkins and Alders 'did something wrong to achieve in their minds something which is right. They are basically not criminals.'

Alders's QC was Alun Talfan Davies, a leading Liberal from a family which is still distinguished and active.

In 1979 Meibion Glyndŵr (Sons of Glyndŵr) began a 12-year arson campaign, with targets being holiday homes, estate agents, boatyards and also politicians – who had letter bombs through the post.

Only one person, a young man from Anglesey, was ever convicted and it was never suggested he was a big player. With more than 200 firebombs in ten years, many of them burning down holiday cottages, the secrecy which protected the 'cells' of bombers was never penetrated by police.

There have been attempts to romanticise and joke about what went on, and to excuse what was happening because it was 'to save Welsh communities'. In fact, it was sheer wickedness. I went to many of the scenes, and it was only by the Grace of God that some victims, including young children, were not burned alive. Experts discovered that an ingredient gave some of the devices a clinging, napalm-type effect.

Just one example of the wickedness was in Moelfre on Anglesey, where a young woman shop assistant picked up an object protruding from the letter box and put it on a wall. It turned out to be a deadly device later made safe.

In December 1989 a device was detonated by the army after being found in a rucksack beneath a parked car outside the Plas y Brenin mountain activities centre in Capel Curig, in the heart of Snowdonia. Had it exploded children and young people could have died.

There was nothing romantic nor heroic about Meibion Glyndŵr. On numerous occasions they were within a hair's breadth of being killers. Nothing romantic nor altruistic either about a group who warned that their principal targets were 'white settlers' in Wales.

In 1993 a man described as 'a foot soldier but not the

organiser' was jailed for having incendiary devices. Two other men were acquitted. It was a trial in Caernarfon at which a succession of MI5 men gave evidence from behind screens – Mr A, Mr B and so on – and denied a dirty tricks campaign. I had always thought that such shadowy figures worked singly. Not so, as many as 30 had been involved.

David Owen, the Chief Constable, hit out afterwards at 'wild and irresponsible allegations' against his men. 'Bombs are made with the sole intention of killing or maiming,' he declared. 'Such behaviour attracts little credit to our nation and all right-thinking people should have no doubt as to their duties to the law and particularly their fellow men, whether they be monolingual or bilingual.'

No one else was ever brought to justice. Perhaps we should be troubled and ashamed that in Wales there are still at large terrorists – because that is what they were – who were prepared to kill and maim. And don't let's forget the earlier terrorist who blew off Ian Cox's foot.

Sometimes I wonder, has Wales had a secret 'Good Friday Agreement' which precludes any action against the perpetrators? A Freedom of Information reply assured me that old crimes were periodically reviewed. But with the mass of forensic evidence which must have accrued, and modern advances in DNA, it seems strange that the bombers still walk free.

14

Saturday night fever

DOING THE LATE shift at the *News of the World* in Manchester, finishing at 3 a.m., involved a long drive back home to Colwyn Bay. But normally, with roads empty, it was completed in 90 minutes.

One night in 1981 I was doing the last round of telephone calls to the main police, fire and ambulance stations in the north-west. The fire brigade in Liverpool told me they were dealing with 'incidents' in Toxteth and that burning cars and petrol bombs seemed to be involved. The police confirmed that there were 'incidents' but could be no more specific.

As it was close to deadline, I remember writing a few paragraphs. Then I decided, despite the late hour, to alert Mercury Press, the main Liverpool Press Agency. It was a call that their boss, Chris Johnson, was later to thank me for effusively. They got a reporter and cameraman on the scene for those early history-making pictures and description of the Toxteth riots, one of the major news stories of the late 20th century.

The following weekend I was in Liverpool when my daughter Alison started a college course. From her building she could see the flames.

In my job you never know when the phone is going to ring to set off another great story. One September afternoon in 1986, on the eve of my daughter Diane's 21st birthday, I had a mysterious call from the London news desk of the *News of the World*. Would I be prepared to drive to a service station on the

M6 in Lancashire, rendezvous with a colleague, Charles Henn, then escort a woman, the focus of a major story, to Southport? I agreed and drove her to the Prince of Wales hotel with her little boy and remained there overnight until relieved by a feature writer.

My task was to guard Monica Coghlan, the prostitute involved when, a week later, the paper famously accused Jeffrey Archer, deputy chairman of the Tory Party, of handing her an envelope 'crammed with £50 notes' via a middleman.

I don't know what other diners made of the unlikely trio sitting at dinner in the Prince of Wales hotel. My brief was to keep her from any other papers, 'particularly the *Sunday Mirror* who know that something's up'.

I found Monica pleasant, and an attentive mum. I'm sure she was a woman to be believed. Sadly, she's now dead.

Among the many tasks on a Saturday night was to catch up with stories in the rival Sunday papers as the first editions arrived. Unfaithful soccer managers, erring MPs and other VIPs became the staple diet. Mainly, however, it was the other papers that had to catch up with the *News of the World*.

At 1 a.m. I got a call from a weekly paper colleague saying that a former star of *Coronation Street*, Jack Howarth who played Albert Tatlock, had died in hospital in Llandudno. It took me ten minutes to confirm it. I knew his son, his next of kin, had been told, and grabbed cuttings from the library and ran the story.

The library in Maxwell House (it was the biggest newspaper office in Europe and in previous lives was called Kemsley House and Thomson House) was shared on a Saturday night by the *News of the World* and *Sunday Mirror*. So it was no surprise when the story also got into the *Mirror*'s final edition.

Then, as now, tales about celebrities, particularly stars from the soaps, were vital for the Sunday pops. And *Coronation Street* being a Manchester show, there were frequent Saturday night visits to their stars to ask, 'Is this true?'

There were crimes and murders, too. Early one Sunday morning, with a photographer, I was first at the scene of a vicious killing alongside a golf course in Hoylake on the Wirral, the victim being the daughter of a judge. And from time to time there were angles to be pursued about the most awful child murders Britain has ever known – those committed by Myra Hindley and Ian Brady. The most compelling and tragic angle was then, and is still today, the whereabouts of their victim Keith Bennett.

The *Sunday Times* claimed that Libyan money was being used to help the miners' strike. So that night I was sent to Barnsley to see Arthur Scargill at his home, accompanied by a photographer. We didn't get to him – a cordon of union heavies surrounding his bungalow ensured that. To me that was an ugly face of Britain and I began to think that Mrs Thatcher was right, and that this man had to be beaten.

It was George McIntosh, then northern editor, who defined for me what in those days, before the cult of celebrity and soaps became the norm, made a good *News of the World* story. 'Old-fashioned French bedroom farce,' he said. I'm sure he was right. Saucy stories were a big seller, and there were plenty of them.

That paper was always the epitome of accuracy. Indeed, in the 1950s the house rule was that the final paragraph of any court story would always repeat the sentence imposed. It would read something like: 'As stated, Jones was sent to prison for two years.' Effective.

My Saturdays in Manchester were to end suddenly in 1986. It happened after Rupert Murdoch achieved his history-making move to the brave new world in Wapping. Incensed, the print unions laid siege. Colleagues in Manchester were called out on strike in support. Stupidly they agreed, and signed their own mass suicide note.

The northern operation had recently switched from Maxwell House, a deal being signed with the *Express* to print instead in that magnificent glass-fronted building in Great Ancoats

Street. Apparently, there was a condition that if production was disrupted beyond a certain number of weeks, the deal could be cancelled...

And that's exactly what happened. Judging that outright opposition was preferable to damage limitation, the print unions refused to work on the *News of the World* in Manchester. They made their point – but a costly one.

I remember seeing a picture of one of the workers kissing the attractive blonde leader of their union, Brenda Dean, herself a Salford girl. Wonder where he got a job after being persuaded to strike?

As I went in the lift to the editorial floor of the *News of the World* on the final Saturday before shut-down, a *Daily Express* sub said to me: 'If Murdoch pulls the plug, who can blame him?' That's what he did. For Manchester as a newspaper centre, it was the beginning of the end. Soon an industry was to virtually disappear from the city.

And Brenda Dean? Later she became a Labour member of the House of Lords, that wonderful and generous place of work. Lately she died. I missed the friendship of great reporters such as Alan Hart, Keith Beabey, Nic Pritchard and Bill Martin. Now the *News of the World* is no more.

On a lighter note – a Fleet Street great once did a door knock at the home of a woman who asked: 'How do I know you're from the *News of the World*?' To which he replied: 'Madam, I have just admitted it.'

15

A date with the Beatles

THE CALL CAME in the middle of a sunny Sunday afternoon in 1967. 'This is ITN here, are you far from Bangor?' 'Half an hour away,' I replied. 'What's up?'

Brian Epstein, manager of the Beatles, had died suddenly. And it so happened that the Beatles, together with other famous members of the Swinging Sixties pop world, including the Rolling Stones and Marianne Faithfull, were in Bangor for a weekend of transcendental meditation with an Indian mystic called Maharishi Mahesh Yogi.

A surreal event it turned out to be. This was in the era of flower power and 'happy drugs'.

When I reached the courtyard outside Bangor Normal College – the last time I'd been there was as a boy when my sister was a student – I was handed a microphone and we waited for the Beatles to emerge for a Press conference. Paul wasn't there. He'd returned hotfoot to London on hearing the news.

I think I was paid about £12 for that interview, which was played on the following night's bulletins. The recording has been heard all over the world, and is also at the Beatles museum in Liverpool. So when I'm dead and gone, my voice will still be heard!

A crowd surrounded myself and Glyn Owen, covering for the BBC, as we did the interviews. Incidentally I first met Glyn when he was a copytaker on the *Daily Post* in Liverpool. He was an opera buff whose clifftop home in Holyhead was packed with old '78' records.

This is how my interview went:

JOHN: *I don't know what to say. We've only just heard, and it's hard to think of things to say. But he was just... he was a warm fellow, you know, and it's terrible.*

Q: *What are your plans now?*
JOHN: *We haven't made any, you know. I mean, we've only just heard.*
RINGO: *Yes, you know – it's as much news to us as it is to everybody else.*

Q: *John, where would you be today without Mr Epstein?*
JOHN (quietly): *I don't know.*

Q: *Are you driving down to London tonight?*
JOHN: *Yes. Somebody's taking us down. Yeah.*

Q: *You heard the news this afternoon I believe, and Paul's already gone down?*
JOHN: *Yes.*

Q: *You've no idea what your plans are for tomorrow?*
JOHN: *No, no. We'll just go and find out, you know. And...*
GEORGE: *Just have to play everything by ear.*

Q: *I understand that Mr Epstein was to be initiated here tomorrow?*
JOHN: *Yes.*

Q: *When was he coming up?*
GEORGE: *Tomorrow... just Monday, that's all we knew.*

Q: *Had you told him very much about the spiritual regeneration movement?*

GEORGE: *Well, as much as we'd learned about spiritualism and various things of that nature, then we tried to pass it on to him. And he was equally as interested as we are, as everybody should be. He wanted to know about life as much as we do.*

Q: *Had you spoken to him since your... since you became interested this weekend?*

JOHN AND RINGO: *No.*

GEORGE: *I spoke to him Wednesday evening, the evening before we first saw Maharishi's lecture – and he was in great spirits.*

Q: *And when did he tell you that he'd like to be initiated?*

GEORGE: *Well, when we arrived here on Friday we got a telephone call later that day to say that Brian would follow us up and be here Monday.*

Q: *Do you intend returning to Bangor before the end of this conference?*

GEORGE: *We probably won't have time now, because Maharishi will only be here till about Thursday and we'll have so much to do in London that we'll have to meet him again some other time.*

Q: *I understand that this afternoon Maharishi conferred with you all. Could I ask you what advice he offered you?*

JOHN: *He told us... uhh... not to get overwhelmed by grief. And whatever thoughts we have of Brian to keep them happy, because any thoughts we have of him will travel to him wherever he is.*

Q: *Had he ever met Mr Epstein?*

JOHN: *No, but he was looking forward to meeting him.*

Q: *Did the Maharishi give you any words of comfort?*

JOHN: *Meditation gives you confidence enough to withstand something like this, even the short amount we've had.*

GEORGE: *There's no such thing as death anyway. I mean, it's death on a physical level, but life goes on everywhere... and you just keep going really. The thing about the comfort is to know that he's OK.*

The most famous group in the world, a sudden death, and meditation... what a mix.

Mind you, not everyone was besotted by the Beatles. A senior magistrate in Rhyl, Councillor Emlyn Williams, feared the visit of John Lennon and Yoko Ono could mean trouble from 'undesirable followers'. The couple was intending to visit Rhyl to help the Hanratty campaign (which I will touch on later), but the councillor feared there would need to be extra police and a cost to the ratepayers. He said: 'I have nothing against the Beatles. They were nice boys when they started but now they want to be authorities on all things.'

Thirty-five years after the Bangor visit, I was invited to a ceremony at the college to commemorate that strange weekend half a lifetime in the past. Someone recalled having said to John Lennon: 'Do you like it in Bangor?' To which he replied: 'Is that where we are?'

I'm afraid the Maharishi didn't register with this cynical Welshman. The Press were invited to meet him. We had to perch on the floor and remove our shoes, presumably in respect. That was unfortunate for Jim Price. He had a massive hole in his sock. I felt it sent a message to the Maharishi.

When Jim died in January 2001 I gave the eulogy at his funeral. A native of Rhayader, he covered north Wales for the *Express* for 28 years. Always with a smile, I don't think he had an enemy in the world. Stories about Jim were legion. Ultimately, with other colleagues, he transferred from the

Express to work on the newborn *Daily Star*. He used to stay in Manchester and spend the night, after the usual hours in the office pub, in a hostelry called the Land of Cakes.

I was told how one night he and a colleague had to share a double bed but, in the early hours, Jim had to get up to relieve himself. While he was away the pub alsatian – described by everyone as the devil dog because of its fierceness – slipped between the sheets. Jim got back in, unaware of the extra company. When they awoke, not a pretty sight after a heavy night, Jim asked his sleeping partner Frank: 'Do you think he fancies you, or me?'

Jim, a farmer's son and Harry Secombe lookalike, told me how when he first joined the *Express* he looked in the correspondents' book and found his name. 'Use for tip-offs only,' was the instruction, 'is a milkman.'

16

Crime and punishment

I'VE SPENT A great deal of my life in courts or involved in reporting crimes. Some of them remain in the mind forever. Within weeks of the Investiture, for instance, a boy of only 14 who went to Sunday school and was studying for a Bible exam stood in the dock at Caernarfon Assizes – within a stone's throw of the castle – accused of the murder of a widow of 73. It was claimed he'd stabbed her because she'd threatened to tell his mother he'd broken into her bungalow.

In Manchester I covered the trial of a pitiless boy of 17 who pushed a caretaker down a city office lift shaft to his death. The judge told him that, had he been a few months older, he could have been hanged.

Sometimes I have marvelled at the bravery and dignity of parents after killers have taken away a loved one. I will always recall the stoicism of Bruce and Pat Cottrill from Old Colwyn whose lovely daughter, schoolteacher Fiona Jones, 26, was randomly killed while she was in France with her husband soon after being married. The French authorities were slow to act, adding to the agony of the parents.

The Cottrills appeared on TV and radio appealing for justice. Eventually they got it in a limited form, but the killer Frederic Blancke, a hospital radiographer, received only 15 years after the ludicrous claim was made that the murder was not premeditated. In fact, after six years he was freed on parole – a mockery of justice. Mrs Thatcher, the Prime Minister, had written, in her own handwriting, a wonderful and obviously heartfelt personal letter giving her support to the Cottrills. It spoke volumes for her humanity.

When eventually an inquest was held, the Cottrills, dignified despite their anger, spoke of their betrayal by the French whose ambassador in London had promised 'a form of words' would be produced which showed that his government recognised there was premeditation.

Even the Queen sent her sympathy. A letter on her behalf stated she had read in the newspapers about Fiona's murder and the subsequent trial. 'Her Majesty has asked me to send her deepest sympathy to you and your family as you seek to come to terms with the loss of your daughter in such dreadful circumstances. Her Majesty can well understand why you have written to her as you did.'

There was the case of a teenage schoolboy from Colwyn Bay, Peter Watts, who one Sunday mysteriously went by train to London, his body then being found in an underpass near Euston station. The mystery was never solved and there were those who were critical about the Scotland Yard inquiry. His distraught father told me he believed life on Earth was the real hell. I've often thought about those words.

Then there was one of the most extraordinary stories in which I've been involved – that of James Hanratty. His father and mother believed passionately that their son did not kill Michael Gregsten in the south of England in 1961, although he was hanged for it. Hanratty had claimed a Rhyl alibi. In 1966, as I trawled the backstreets of Rhyl following up a *Panorama* report on the BBC, I found two women, Mrs Margaret Walker and Mrs Ivy Vincent, who seemed to back the alibi and had made relevant statements to the police at the time. In his book *Who Killed Hanratty?* the investigative journalist Paul Foot referred to me kindly as 'an enterprising freelance journalist from Llandudno'.

I met Det. Chief Supt. Doug Nimmo, head of Manchester CID, when he journeyed to Rhyl to open a second inquiry into the alibi claim. He told me he could not understand why Hanratty, in the shadow of the noose, should have made some statements which were obvious lies when his life was at stake. A strong point, obviously.

James Hanratty senior and his wife came to Rhyl to head a campaign to clear their son posthumously. It was moving to hear his father, so convinced of his boy's innocence, referring to him not as James, but his surname 'Hanratty'. 'Hanratty was not the killer, he was in Rhyl at the time,' he insisted. It had taken over the couple's lives. He declared: 'My son may have taken a watch or a car but, believe me, he was never a murderer.' The Hanrattys were helped, gratis I believe, by a campaigning solicitor I had first met when working in Wallasey – Barney Berkson.

More than 30 years later the advent of DNA was to tell a different story. I spoke to Paul Foot just before he died and asked what progress was being made in the campaign. 'It's not looking good,' he replied.

Guilty or innocent, the Hanratty affair did have one positive outcome in my view: by helping to sway opinion which had led to the abolition of hanging. It was strange that Rhyl should also have an involvement in the other emotional cause célèbre which helped to rid Britain of the gallows for ever – the execution of Ruth Ellis. Rhyl was her birthplace.

My own view on capital punishment was influenced by Cassandra, that wonderful polemicist who graced the *Daily Mirror*, a former advertising copywriter who I regard as the greatest columnist in my lifetime. It was the magnificent essay he wrote on the day that Ruth Ellis was hanged, describing the hideous ritual of what would happen. 'The Woman They Hang Today' I think was the banner headline, and it occupied the entire front page. Tabloid journalism at its best. Brilliant, opinion-forming journalism.

Tabloid journalism has many detractors. Self-righteous and often snobbish critics use the word with a sneer. Then I think of William Connor (Cassandra) and the words that, I'm sure, were pivotal in making the hangman a figure of the past. A victory of epic proportions for tabloid journalism.

There was courage from the father of the killer of seven-year-old Sophie Hook, taken from a tent in her uncle's garden in Llandudno and murdered. Howard Hughes' father took the noble but heartbreaking course of telling police that his son had confessed to him.

At the end of the trial at Chester Crown Court Mr Justice Curtis, who handed out three life terms, thanked the Press 'for ensuring this man has had a fair trial'. Det. Supt. Eric Jones, who was in charge of the inquiry, said to us: 'Thank you for the restraint throughout the inquiry and the trial. As far as we as an investigating team are concerned, I can only describe you as magnificent.'

Alas, such a rapport between senior detectives and journalists covering major crimes has all but disappeared following the disaster of Leveson. Journalists no longer have the contacts, the police have lost an ally. All to placate celebrities and those who hate the popular Press.

Information, such as it is, is doctored then channelled through a Press Office. Propaganda rather than news is often the norm. Nowadays journalists have little contact with detectives – and don't even know their names. I have letters in which three CID chiefs, on their retirement, express gratitude for co-operation and friendship through the years. What is sometimes forgotten by modern police chiefs is that we are both on the same side and that publicity can be an immense help in solving crimes. I know of cases solved not by the police – but by journalists.

Howard Hughes, convicted in 1996 of the appalling murder of little Sophie Hook, had six years earlier been accused of indecently assaulting two young girls at a block of flats near Llandudno Hospital. Magistrates decided it was so serious that a judge should hear the case at the crown court. But the girls were aged only five and three, there was no medical or forensic evidence, and the next time he appeared in court on remand the magistrates were told it was being dropped. It was an appalling case, with one girl being attacked and her underwear removed on the stairwell, and the other girl allegedly being held by the bottom.

In 1986 he was accused of assaulting a nine-year-old girl in Colwyn Bay, but the parents of the girl were unwilling for the case to go ahead. A few days before the murder of Sophie he'd been fined for having a knife. Somehow there seemed an appalling logic leading up to the savage murder. It was a crime waiting to happen.

The crimes that are most horrible, it goes without saying, are those in which children are the victims. Another was the murder of ten-year-old Jane Taylor of Mobberley in Cheshire. She vanished on her bike in 1966 and her remains were found six years later buried in a wood in Llanfairfechan, where her killer had driven with her body.

A ten-year-old boy had found human remains protruding from the soil when he took a walk in the woods. When such finds are made the first possibility is that the body is that of a tramp. But not in this case. When I saw the Chief Constable of North Wales at the scene, the genial Philip Myers, I realised that this was something deeply sinister. He took me aside and said the following day could see startling developments, and that the body in the shallow grave was that of a young person.

A school dental chart identified Jane. Ironically, the little boy who had found the remains was from Bollington, not so far from Jane's home.

Soon the head of North Wales CID, Anthony Clarke, was joined by his counterpart from Cheshire, Arthur Benfield. Dozens of police officers combed the woods for clues and a massive manhunt began. Eventually the pieces fell into place and the killer was arrested. In Mobberley there is now the Jane Taylor Memorial Park.

I will never forget Christmas Eve 1984. I had a call from an inspector who could hardly contain himself. 'Derek,' he said, 'get in your car and go to Tywyn court. When you get there you won't believe what you hear. It involves a chapel minister.'

I tipped off my friend Barry Michael Jones, then working for HTV, and Eryl Jones-Williams who covered for the *Cambrian News* in Dolgellau, and drove 65 miles to the little court which adjoined the police station. There the Rev. Emyr Owen, a Welsh Presbyterian minister, faced three charges of mutilating bodies, and one of a threat to kill. The problem was the charges were not put in court. We eventually persuaded the court clerk to release them, after he'd driven the chairwoman to her home. 'This is going to ruin Christmas in Tywyn,' he said, pleading with us to treat it sensitively. I recorded, with some difficulty, a piece for Radio Wales, then drove back home.

On Christmas Day I phoned (yes phoned, because computers were not yet being used for data transmission) the story to every national paper. Some of the copytakers found the story hard to believe (as indeed it was). One news desk rang back and asked: 'Is this really true – you had a drink, Derek?' When the case came to Caernarfon Crown Court, prosecuting barrister (later judge) Huw Daniel remarked: 'This case is unusual to say the least.' He would not include dates in the details, 'specifically to take into account public disquiet'. In other words, to protect families whose loved ones could have been affected.

A couple of years earlier Owen, who I described as a Norman Wisdom lookalike, had sat in the same court as chaplain to the High Sheriff of Gwynedd. Couples whose babies he'd baptised wondered whether to have another ceremony, and those at whose marriages he'd officiated winced – including a prominent broadcaster who excluded herself from reporting the case.

Owen's signature in a New Testament, which he'd given to a young man who'd belonged to one of his chapels, was the giveaway. Police discovered it matched the handwriting on anonymous letters which had been circulating. Detective Constable Gwyn Roberts went to see him at the manse about the letters and his 'copper's intuition', as he described it, persuaded him to make a search. It was then that horrific, incriminating slides and tapes – in English and Welsh – were discovered which revealed the depth of the minister's depravity. Eventually, in 1985, he was jailed for four years. Detective Constable Roberts handled his inquiries so sensitively that no family was ever aware that a loved one might have been the victim of the parson's mutilations.

The most wicked killer? Equal first must be the gay Peter Moore, north Wales's only serial murderer, and Howard Hughes who killed Sophie Hook.

Evil Moore killed four men – bachelor Henry Roberts, 56, a retired railway porter of Caergeiliog, Anglesey; Edward Carthy, 28, of Birkenhead, whose body was found in Clocaenog Forest, near Ruthin; Keith Randles, 49, a safety manager from Chester, found stabbed at an Anglesey construction site and butchered by the roadside in a random killing; and Tony Davies, 40, of Llysfaen, near Colwyn Bay, stabbed on the beach in Abergele.

Mr Randles was the only victim who wasn't gay. Moore loved publicity and he appeared on TV and claimed credit for bringing the cinema back to Holyhead, Bagillt, Denbigh and Blaenau Ffestiniog.

Several young women reporters who interviewed him one-to-one still shudder...

Even when brought to trial, Moore – called the most dangerous man in Wales by prosecutor Alex Carlile QC – was prepared to milk the publicity. When he arrived at Colwyn Bay court for remand hearings he would pose – yes pose – for the cameramen outside.

In a perspex-fronted cell at Walton Prison it was said he'd been caged alongside Howard Hughes and a double child killer so that they could be watched 24 hours a day.

Moore claimed that killing 'made me feel better'. At his home were found several dozen watches – believed to have been taken as souvenirs. But to whom did they belong?

In 1994 a 33-year-old man from Abergele was locked up on remand, charged with the abduction of a hitch-hiker aged 24 in the Conwy Valley and committing a horrendous sex offence against him. Just before he was to be sent to the crown court, the Crown Prosecution Service realised he was not responsible and dropped the case.

'The family are concerned that the perpetrator of the crime is still around,' declared his solicitor, Niclas Parry (now a crown court judge). 'People have no idea what the case has done to them, they've lost thousands of pounds and their home and have had to move out of north Wales.'

Another terrible murder was that of 90-year-old widow Mabel Leyshon in her bungalow in Menai Bridge. She was the victim of 'vampire' killer Mathew Hardman, 17, who lived nearby and used to deliver her papers. It was said at his trial that she'd been stabbed to death and her heart had been removed as part of a ritual. The boy, studying A level art, got a minimum of 12 years.

As the rector of Llanfair P.G., the Rev. Robert Townsend, put it: 'There is no real answer to the question: why did it happen? For the healing process to really start we need to know why it happened and what was the motivation. We may never know and in that case there's going to be a deep scar in the community which will take years to go away.'

Hardman's pals said he liked dance music and heavy metal. The only clue was that after his father's death he became obsessed by that which was morbid – and by death.

A murder in the Conwy Valley involved a Korean alleged killer and an English rose. In 1998 Jong Yoon Rhee got life for the murder of his pretty young wife Natalie in a fire at a holiday cottage near Llanrwst.

Natalie, 34, the privately educated daughter of a retired Air Commodore, had been swept off her feet by the smooth talking and sophisticated son of an academic. Rhee, with at least £90,000 gambling debts from London casinos, set fire to the holiday cottage they were renting in the hope that he could obtain £250,000 life insurance according to the prosecution. His wife's charred body was found in a bedroom.

But Rhee wasn't to escape a murder conviction – thanks to the painstaking Det. Supt. John Williams and his team. Recently, after serving 18 years, Rhee has been released from prison and deported to South Korea, protesting his innocence. His story is that he climbed out of a window first, then waited to catch his pregnant wife, but she never jumped.

The year 1992 got off to a gruesome start when Denise Reynolds, 39, was knifed to death by her estranged husband Vernon who burst into a New Year's Eve party in Llandudno. Then he drove ten miles in the family's Morris Ital car to the Conwy Valley where he crashed head-on with another car, killing three young men and himself. I still think of that tragedy when I pass the spot near Talycafn.

Drugs have been the cause of much misery and crime, and this continues. Even some of our loveliest towns have been targeted. In 1996 I was at Chester Crown Court when five men were jailed for running a drugs den 'almost like a departmental store' in the middle of Ruthin. An undercover detective had been told 'buy half an ounce of cannabis and you get a free bar of chocolate'. When a flat inside the Crown House was raided, piles of chocolate bars were discovered.

A police helicopter hovering above spotted smoke billowing from a chimney as the criminals tried to burn cannabis on a stove. Like a scene from an American movie, an SAS-style raid was mounted with a crane used so that police could swarm through windows. The building was guarded by two sets of sliding gates and monitored by closed-circuit TV. Youngsters queued for drugs, and inside were found LSD, ecstasy and cannabis. Five men were jailed for between three and seven years. Judge Sir Robin David QC said they'd operated 'like a cancer in the rural town of Ruthin and were doing great damage to the welfare of young people'. I have little time for those who urge that cannabis should be made legal. If they had spent the time in court that I have, they'd have heard scores of

Derek, aged 3, in front of Eirias Park pavilion, Colwyn Bay

Derek, aged 12, with his sister Joan

The long and short… with Trevor Williams, esteemed *Weekly News* reporter in Colwyn Bay

North Wales Ironmongers' dinner at Rhos Abbey Hotel, 1952. With Trevor Williams of the *Weekly News* and Ron Fawcett of the *Llandudno Advertiser*.

National Service with the Royal Marines

A Company, No. 823 Squad, July 1952. Derek's on the bottom right, looking glum and feeling it!

Off-duty moment in Port Fouad, 1953

At the 1957 Miss New Brighton final with the *Daily Post*'s Allan Robinson, the *Daily Sketch*'s Freddie Aspden, and (in light jacket) freelance John Brindle, Derek's best man

Derek with his Hillman Minx in Manchester, 1960

Recalling *Daily Herald* times in 1963; in foreground, Geoff Levy, later *Daily Mail* stalwart, and visiting Gay Byrne, Irish TV personality

Peter Thomas QC MP, later Lord Thomas of Gwydir, at the National Eisteddfod in Llandudno, 1963 – the first Welshman to become Tory party chairman

© John Lawson-Reay

The Queen Mother on a private visit to Bodnant Gardens in the Conwy Valley in 1964

© John Lawson-Reay

Derek in conversation with John Lennon in Bangor after the death of Brian Epstein, 1967

© John Lawson-Reay

'Fab Four' in north Wales, 1967

© John Lawson-Reay

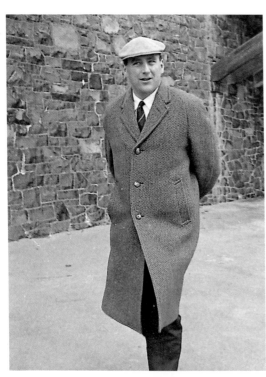

Crombie overcoat and cap stylish in 1967, yes. But not really appropriate at the scene of a shipwreck! It was a Sunday morning, maybe diverted from church!

© John Lawson-Reay

Ednyfed Hudson Davies MP, 1970

© John Lawson-Reay

Harold Wilson and his wife Mary at the Winter Gardens, Llandudno, 1972

© John Lawson-Reay

Wyn Roberts, son of the manse. The Welsh politician credited with doing more than anyone for the Welsh language.

© John Lawson-Reay

Sir Anthony Meyer, the 'stalking horse' who stood against Margaret Thatcher in 1989. With wife Barbadee in Colwyn Bay.

© John Lawson-Reay

Richard Williams and his Welsh pound notes, 1980

© John Lawson-Reay

Specimen note of the original "Black Sheep Bank", as the Aberystwyth and Tregaron Bank Ltd was popularly known.

It was one of the early drovers banks.

When the "Chief Treasury of Wales Ltd" changed its name to "The Black Sheep Company of Wales" it drew on this past history and was careful to remain a Treasury and not a Bank, thus avoiding many of the rules governing banks.
Treasury Notes, known as Bradbury's were issued in Britain in the early 1920's and withdrawn, although collectors still have some in their collections.
The change of name prompted a headline in the "Times" of "A Black Sheep in Bank's clothing".
The Treasury has, despite the displeasure of the British Government, always had an U.S.Dollar account in the United States of America. With the abolition of the Exchange Control Regulations, it now has a U.S.Dollar account with the National Westminster Bank Ltd, Craig y don, Llandudno.

28/3/80

The words of Richard Williams, banker extraordinaire

Gwmni y Ddafad Ddu Gymreig • **Cyfyngedig**

Post Office Box 8,
Colwyn Bay, Clwyd,
Wales

Cables: "Computers Llandudno"
Telephone: Glan Conway 751

GYNT, PRIF TRYSORFA CYMRU CYFYNGEDIG
(Chief Treasury of Wales Limited)

PRESS RELEASE - EMBARGOED UNTIL 8th APRIL 1980

The Black Sheep of Wales sells to the World.

At the Incentive Marketing Exhibition commencing at Brighton on April 12th 1980 Welsh Pound Treasury Notes will be introduced to several hundred of the World's top advertising and promotion agencies by Coinette (Currency) Ltd, of Tiptree, Colchester, Essex (Managing Director Mr Stan G.Bacon) by one of the only two such companies in the World specialising in this type of activity.

Companies who have previously used their products include large motor companies; finance; paint; chemical; chocolate; oil; hotels; newspaper and news media; tobacco; breakfast food; tyres; photocopying; chemists;insurance and engineering.

The Agencies with whom Coinette have happily worked include some of the largest in the world, who will be represented in Brighton.

Two special Welsh Treasury Pound Notes have been produced for this purpose, based on the original Black Sheep Bank Note. Several thousand have been made available for the Exhibition as specimen samples.

Contact. . Coinette (Currency) Ltd. Stan G.Bacon. 0621 815563
Treasury. Richard Williams. 0496 0492 68 751

Director: E. E. Williams.   Secretary: John ap Richard
Registered Office: Brynrhedyn Farm, Glan Conway, Gwynedd.
Registered in Great Britain No. 941507

Those wonderful Welsh banknotes

Llandudno's magnificent Pier Pavilion burned down in 1994. There is still a black hole where it once stood so proudly.

© John Lawson-Reay

Holiday cottage destroyed by firebombers in Cwm Penmachno

© John Lawson-Reay

The late, great Jim Price, ex-*Daily Express* and close friend who didn't have an enemy in the world

Legendary *Daily Post* columnist and friend Ivor Wynne Jones

Heyday in Old Budget Gate – note typewriter available, just in case!

'Old Hacks' Christmas get-together

Journalist Glyn Bellis after taking to the air with Prince William's former colleagues at RAF Valley

Nigel Bellis behind the camera

At Buckingham Palace in 2009 when Shirley received her MBE from Prince Charles – Alison and Diane were there for Shirley's big day

Enjoying an East Sussex break with Shirley

With their children at diamond wedding celebrations in 2017

Still winning awards: Scoop of the Year finalist at the Wales Media Awards, 2016

The good life – living it up mid-Atlantic aboard *Queen Mary 2*

tales of men and women whose lives, and sometimes sanity, have been ruined by the drug, scarred even from childhood. If it were made even more available, on open sale, the result would be catastrophic. Now, of course, heroin and cocaine are brought to seaside towns and rural communities, organised by Mr Bigs in north-west cities, producing misery and crime. And other mind-blowing concoctions render those who buy them senseless.

17

Great characters

RICHARD WILLIAMS WAS a genius, but a flawed one. The 53-year-old former bank clerk claimed to have invented the magnetic encoding used on cheques. Unfortunately, he'd failed to take out a patent. So when he shocked an irascible county court judge who asked him to list his assets and he replied '14 million pounds, owed by the clearing banks', it wasn't strictly true.

He formed a company called the 'Chief Treasury of Wales', but was asked by the Board of Trade to change it because it was 'misleading'. So he renamed it the 'Black Sheep Company of Wales', after a bank which existed in mid Wales in the early 1800s.

His notes had the symbol of a lamb for ten shillings, a sheep for £1, a ram for £5 and two rams for £10.

Richard Williams opened a 'shop' in a terrace house in Deganwy to sell 'Welsh treasury notes'. 'It's everyone's dream to print his own money,' he declared. He turned them out on a machine, like an episode from a comedy. On the windows were notices proclaiming: 'Welsh Treasury Notes Exchanged Here. Business Hours 1.30–2.30 p.m.'

He sold them at face value and put the cash in a deposit account at a clearing bank – which made him six per cent interest and so, he said, secured the integrity of his new currency. I will never forget him turning the handle of a machine which spewed the fresh notes on to a table, as he said, printing his own money. A Treasury spokesman, when asked for a response, said: 'No comment.' The Inland Revenue mistakenly allowed their Liverpool Impress Office to put an official stamp on ten shilling and one pound notes. 'I am to express the Board's regret for this error,' explained a later letter, quaintly referring to such arcane law as Section 30 of the Wales and Berwick on Tweed Act, 1746. But to his delight hundreds of the notes, bearing the Impress stamp, were already in circulation, acquiring an additional novelty value.

When he got a letter from the Board of Trade instructing him to change the name of his company, the Chief Treasury of Wales Ltd., within six weeks because 'it gives a misleading indication of the nature of its activities as to be likely to harm the public,' Mr Williams replied, cheekily, that he would do so but they wouldn't be holding a board meeting for another three weeks. 'With the new title it may be necessary to put on the notes the words "Formerly Chief Treasury of Wales Ltd.",' he explained.

He produced a million pound note for the benefit of an Arab potentate, and many of his notes are still to be seen today at auctions. He also produced his own Welsh five shilling notes – calling them the Welsh greenbacks. The Lord Chamberlain complained that some of the notes 'bear a heraldic device resembling the Arms of the Prince of Wales'.

Thirty years before computers became a way of life, Richard Williams had a company called Computer Consultants. He used to collect redundant giant machines and take out the valuable metals. Richard Williams was the sort of man whose cleverness and quirky ideas would have been a gift to British intelligence. He had immense confidence in his own ability and ideas, and despite the setbacks could not be deterred.

He also had a knack for attracting publicity and of putting the authorities on the back foot. When he staged an exhibition in Llandudno, he arranged to borrow from NASA the computer which was used to guide Apollo 11 to the moon. It failed to arrive – so he reported it missing to Scotland Yard. Then it was discovered, having been mislaid at Heathrow for 15 hours. 'It got Apollo 11 to the moon twelve seconds late but to Llandudno two days late,' pointed out Mr Williams, with ever an eye for a good quote. Another exhibit was a tiny piece of the shield from a Gemini spacecraft, charred by the heat of re-entry.

Computer pioneers from throughout the world gave lectures he organised at a conference in the Grand Hotel in Llandudno, including a woman Admiral from the US Navy, but Mr Williams was disappointed that so few people turned up at a hundred guineas a time. Sixty bought tickets and Mr Williams, as ever undeterred, said: 'I'm happy I've recovered my costs, I was not going to become a millionaire.'

Eventually he retired to a fish farm in the Conwy Valley. He was one of the most amazing people I ever met. And he had that knack of being one step ahead of officialdom, making them look ponderous and silly. At one stage he really did add insult to injury for the Bank of England – his 'Welsh' pound notes were fetching a greater value than sterling in the USA.

I've always admired those who are prepared to take on authority and even the State, and particularly those with a sense of humour, like Allan Jones who used to be postmaster and grocer in Frongoch, a village near Bala where, incidentally, hundreds of Irish rebels were interned during the First World War.

Outside his shop was a six feet tall, green and white sign – which was discussed once at a magistrates' court, twice in quarter sessions, and once in the high court. Finally, after 15 months, he was cleared of displaying the sign without planning permission. The 'authorities' had objected because, as well as advertising the shop, it also proclaimed 'Bed and Breakfast', 'Cups of Tea', and 'Fishing Permits'.

As he argued, in a tourist area it was vital to provide a service for holidaymakers. He'd been fined £2 by magistrates, but this was quashed by the quarter sessions which ruled the sign was on part of what were business premises. But then came a major blow, with the high court upholding an appeal by Merioneth County Council and sending the case back to the quarter sessions.

Feisty Mr Jones fought on. He produced six witnesses to point out that there had been signs at the spot for the previous half-century, well before the planning regulations came into force in 1948. That was it, game set and match to plucky Allan Jones, who rightly wanted to know how much it had all cost. 'In the low hundreds, nothing like a thousand pounds,' replied Merioneth County Council, loftily. But then, it wasn't their money to squander, just that of the ratepayers. Nothing changes, does it?

I must admit that I have been sometimes unimpressed by Welsh-language campaigners, because humour doesn't seem to be their forte. But an exception bears the wonderful name of Ffred Ffransis, son-in-law of the late Gwynfor Evans, Plaid Cymru's first MP. Whenever Ffred was involved in a demonstration, it was with good humour. When he was a student in Aberystwyth he went on hunger strike at his lodgings in Bow Street.

He lay on a bed, Ghandi-like. As I entered, his landlord took me aside. 'I'm sorry about the smell, Mr Bellis, but Ffred is dehydrating,' he explained. Dehydrating or not, Ffred was able to give me a good story for the *Sunday Mirror* and agreed to a picture.

There was an amazing, supremely confident character called Tom Munson, a painter and decorator who was certain he could end the fuel crisis. He wrote to Prime Minister Edward Heath seeking help to market 'Munson's Mixture' as it was dubbed, containing 95 per cent distilled water and other ingredients which were a close secret.

The formula, he said, had been given to him by a German POW after it had been tried in the Western Desert. 'What I've done is to mix oil and water to produce a combustible fuel, something the scientists said could never be done. The water is heated to 47 degrees and then cooled to almost freezing before the additive is poured on. Most of the ingredients could be

117

bought by a housewife with her weekly shopping,' he said. 'I could be on my way to a fortune.'

Munson said the major oil companies were worried about his invention. But then, mysteriously, he disappeared from the scene.

And there was Bob Renphrey, the 'walking calamity'. He even wrote a book about his disasters on Friday the 13th, including car crashes, being knocked down by a motorbike, walking through a plate-glass shop window (and getting the bill), throwing a stick for his dog which injured his wife, and being made redundant as a bus conductor.

Bob, who lived in Barmouth and then moved to Penmaenmawr, was for the benefit of radio and TV always willing to stay in bed on Friday the 13th.

When he died in 1998 his wife Betty wanted to arrange the funeral on Friday the 13th – but had to wait until the following Monday. I suppose that was bad luck, too. Betty said that Bob, who'd fought a brave battle against cancer, never lost his sense of humour. 'I'm sure he'd have liked his funeral to be on Friday the 13th. It would have crowned it for Bob,' she added.

Another great character was Jess Yates, organist-turned famous TV presenter and producer. My first meetings with Jess were unhappy, seeking with my colleagues to obtain his reaction after being fired from *Stars on Sunday* because of his love affair with a blonde beauty called Anita Kay, 31 years his junior. 'Bishop and the Showgirl' was how the *News of the World* broke the story.

Stars on Sunday was a TV programme watched by millions, and by some viewers Jess was looked upon as being as religiously important as the Archbishop of Canterbury. Put in biblical terms, Yorkshire Television cast Jess into the wilderness, and he had no work for the rest of his life.

He blamed Hughie Green for having tipped off the paper and wrecking his career. Luckily, Jess was dead when it was later revealed that the hated Green, not Jess, was proved by DNA to be the father of Paula Yates. (I once met Green, who recounted how during the war he used to ferry Catalina flying boats from Canada to Beaumaris in Anglesey – laden with contraband whisky which was later rowed ashore in small boats. I have never met a man who swore so constantly.)

Before he died, Jess and I became good friends. Indeed at one time we had planned to set up a production company, but it never happened.

On the day he was sacked he had four network shows but his employers were unforgiving. Perhaps Jess should have taken them to an industrial tribunal. These days he'd have probably won. One newspaper supported Jess throughout – the *Daily Express*. It couldn't stand the hypocrisy.

At his funeral in April 1993 – he is buried in a family grave at the Great Orme cemetery – Bob Geldof held the hand of his wife Paula Yates as he joined the 30 mourners. A local curate, the Rev. John Powell, in his address called Jess 'a Llandudno son' and said he'd helped youngsters to stardom 'and made a major contribution to religious broadcasting with *Stars on Sunday.*'

Another imperturbable character was Esmé Kirby, devoting much of her life to defending Snowdonia, who died in her sleep aged 89 in 1999 at her lonely mountainside home, Dyffryn Mymbyr. She was founder chairwoman of the Snowdonia National Park Society, and after she was ousted after many years, undeterred she set up the Esmé Kirby Snowdonia Trust.

Her first husband, who later lived in Japan, was Thomas Firbank, author of the autobiographical bestseller *I Bought a Mountain* in which she was the young wife and heroine. Later she married Major Peter Kirby, who until retirement was curator of the Royal Welch Fusiliers Museum at Caernarfon Castle. They were married for almost half a century, farming 3,000 acres on the side of the rugged Glyder Range.

One of her biggest victories was to save the historic Cromlech Boulders beside the Llanberis Pass from being blown up to widen the road. A workman was actually drilling holes for the explosives when she got the work stopped. The boulders had been there since the Ice Age and Esmé wasn't prepared to let 20th-century councillors destroy them.

One of her passions was to preserve the red squirrel – and a few days after her death she was to have attended a symposium about it.

18

A strange tragedy
in the hills

HIPPY MICHAEL DAWE, 28, died a strange death in a remote cottage in one of the loveliest valleys of Wales after eating salad which contained hemlock water dropwort – described as the most dangerous and poisonous plant in Britain.

It happened in 1974 in the Pennant Valley, near Porthmadog, of which the Welsh poet Eifion Wyn wrote: 'Why Lord do you make Cwm Pennant so beautiful – when a shepherd's life is so short?'

Poor Michael Dawe's life was short, too, ending after he ate the deadly concoction, though another man and a young woman recovered. A native of Ilford who had emigrated to Australia and then returned to Britain, he belonged to a sect known as the Children of God, and the three of them read the Bible and lived off the earth.

All had been taken to hospital with convulsions. Dawe had died from asphyxia due to the collapse of his lungs.

Maria del Carmen Neif, 25, who came from Curaçao, said Dawe was known as 'Paul, Apostle' and they were 'married – but not legally'.

She explained: 'We lived entirely by faith. We preached the word to the world and anyone who was in need of spiritual help.'

Welshman Gareth Jenkins, 24, a Buddhist, added: 'We lived

a very simple life. We have very strong spiritual aspirations which is the reason why I lived there. It is a very peaceful place, very inspiring.'

Dawe had a knowledge of plants and had brought back to the cottage one which resembled a parsnip and was 'quite juicy and attractive'. But it was also fatal.

Maria, who afterwards went to live at the London headquarters of the Children of God, remarked: 'Paul was just ready to go and God has taken him. It has made my outlook a lot stronger after seeing what the Lord did.'

Snowdonia is often the scene of sudden death, usually in falls from cliffs. But there had never been one quite like the demise of Michael Dawe – 'Paul, Apostle'.

19

Sea rescues

In 2009 THERE were events held at the Anglesey village of Moelfre to mark the 150th anniversary of the loss of the *Royal Charter*, a steam-powered sailing ship cast on to the rocks in a 100 mph storm.

It was one of Britain's most tragic shipwrecks – and the most dramatic story NOT to have been made into a Hollywood blockbuster. She was on her way from Melbourne to Liverpool laden with gold, and of the 452 passengers and crew, including families, only 39 survived. Most of them owed their lives to the 'Moelfre 28' – local men who formed a human chain as the 2,700-ton ship broke up. It was claimed that some of those aboard had stuffed their pockets with gold dust as they tried to get to shore.

By coincidence the anniversary coincided with 50 years since the rescue in 1959 of the eight-man crew from the 500-ton Cardiff coaster *Hindlea*, driven ashore at Moelfre in an identical storm. The late Richard Evans, coxswain of the village lifeboat, gained the first of his two gold medals – 'the lifeboat VC'.

His second came a few years later in 1966 when he and his crew saved those aboard the *Nafsipiros*, a Greek freighter which was drifting towards rocks off the Skerries, near Holyhead, again in a huge gale. I remember listening on a coastguard radio as the ship drifted closer and closer to disaster – while arguments went on over which international tug company could be offered salvage rights. At one stage the lifeboat was swept on to the heaving deck of the *Nafsiporos*, only for another wave to wash it off. Among the lifeboat crew was a retired master of an *Empress* liner – Capt. David Jeavons. Holyhead lifeboat shared in the drama.

The legendary Dick Evans was in tears on the day he said goodbye to his beloved lifeboat on his 65th birthday. The RNLI arranged a special ceremony for Dick, a lifeboatman for 49 years and cox at Moelfre for 16. Fittingly there was a gale! The lifeboat was lowered just a few yards down the slipway so that Dick could stand in the bows and receive the acclaim of his admirers. He thanked his faithful crew. 'Never once have these boys ever quibbled or in any way doubted my decisions, that is something of which I'm very proud,' he said. Among telegrams wishing him well was one from the crew of the *Nafsiporos*, whose lives he'd saved.

One of the most colourful rescues in north Wales involved a great character called Jack Williams, skipper of a Conwy trawler. There is a memorial plaque on the quayside in Conwy from where he sailed for many years.

Twenty-stone Jack took his 49-ton *Kilravock* into Llandudno bay in May 1968 to end a crisis. Nearly 400 American tourists, on a cruise aboard the luxury liner *Kungsholm*, were being ferried back to their ship aboard the pleasure steamer *St Trillo* when she broke down. Despite a 50 mph gale and big seas, Jack managed to get a line aboard the *St Trillo* and towed her to Llandudno pier. The relieved Americans spent the night in three Llandudno hotels before being taken to Liverpool by coach next day to rejoin the *Kungsholm* for their expensive 'spring adventure cruise'.

For Jack, a wartime minesweeper skipper, there was a giant bottle of Bourbon which he shared with his five-man crew.

One of the most amazing sea escapes in north Wales was that of angler Brian Turner, 34, a six-feet-tall steel erector from Lancashire, who in October 1969 spent an 18-hour nightmare clinging to an upturned speedboat in the choppy Irish Sea. He'd vainly tried to save his two friends as they clung to the

124

upside-down boat in the moonlight but, exhausted, they had slipped off. As soon as he pulled one back on board, the other slid into the water. A trawler had passed within 200 yards but in the darkness failed to see them.

Eventually, Rhyl lifeboat spotted the speedboat showing only six inches above the waves, and saw an arm waving weakly at them. Rhyl lifeboat secretary Jack Owen said: 'It's a miracle he's alive. The speedboat must have drifted 20 miles.'

Sgt. Hugh Morgan, navigator of an RAF rescue helicopter which flew the survivor to hospital in Rhyl, said: 'He's the luckiest man in Britain.' They'd set off from Rhos-on-Sea on a Sunday afternoon fishing trip – but had no lifejackets or flares. The alarm was raised by relatives at 4.30 next morning.

In 1980 four men from the Warrington area, going angling from Conwy, drowned after making two fatal errors – trying to cut across shallow water instead of using the main channel, and not wearing lifejackets. Their cabin cruiser hit a sandbank and turned over. An inshore lifeboat was at the scene in three minutes, but they'd been swept away. Another illustration of the perils of taking risks at sea.

In 1991 ten men were lost and two survived when their ship went down in a 70 mph gale with 30ft waves, 16 miles south of Holyhead. Rescuers described conditions as horrendous. The two Polish survivors from the 1,876-ton Maltese-registered tanker *Kimya*, en route to Birkenhead from Spain with a cargo of sunflower oil, clung to their buoyancy aids for two hours and owed their lives to radio beacons on their lifejackets which guided an RAF helicopter towards them.

The captain was Norwegian and other members of the crew Polish, Portuguese and Ghanian. After treatment for hypothermia the two survivors were able to leave hospital – lucky men who will never forget that wild winter's night in the Irish Sea.

In November 2011 Prince William, based at RAF Valley, was at the controls of a helicopter which in the middle of the night went to the scene of an almost identical tragedy in the same area in a storm. Six Russian crewmen drowned but two were saved by his Sea King crew from the huge seas after the stone-carrying *Swanland* broke apart. The Russian Ambassador sent a letter of thanks to the Prince and rescuers.

On the quayside in Conwy is a memorial to three men lost in their trawler *Katy* which sank mysteriously when returning from Red Wharf Bay, Anglesey, in early 1994. It's believed that she'd been swamped in rough weather. A marine inquiry heard that it was 'probably a very rapid sinking'. The bodies of skipper Gary Hughes, 30, Lee Rowlands, 22, and Robert Hall, 21, have never been found.

And there's a memorial on Llandudno promenade to four young men, two of them brothers, and a woman who drowned in 1992 when their speedboat capsized on a fishing trip. Just one, 19-year-old Richard Shenouda, survived, picked up after a two-hour swim.

In 1991 a plaque was unveiled in Rhosneigr on Anglesey to mark an appalling tragedy during the dark days of the Second World War. Eleven would-be rescuers had drowned in raging seas, together with the three-man crew of an aircraft, a Botha, which ditched less than a mile offshore just after taking off from RAF Valley to aid a convoy which was under attack. A local policeman and a coastguard were among those who gave their lives when four rescue boats capsized trying to reach the plane. The plaque was erected after a campaign by Arthur Jones, 61, who was only 12 when his father Evan, a coastguard, perished while trying to save others. Just one man had survived.

When I started freelancing in 1963 my first phone call was to the rescue helicopter squadron at Valley. My admiration for generations of those crews – and particularly the pilots and winchmen – is unbounded. I have written hundreds of stories about their bravery on land and sea. How wonderful that when, in 1991, a Luftwaffe pilot, *Hauptman* Berend Neuen (known as Bernie to his colleagues), returned to Germany he'd taken part in 150 rescues and saved many lives. He was on an exchange scheme and was presented with a special badge by the station commander to mark 3,000 hours at the controls of a Wessex helicopter. His worst moment had been the Lockerbie tragedy which he said was an experience he will never forget. Great, though, that the once-dreaded Luftwaffe should send a pilot to join with the RAF in that noble task of saving lives. Now the helicopter rescue service has been partially privatised and we no longer get first-hand accounts of the bravery of those who save the lives of victims of the sea and mountains, which is wrong and an injustice to those heroes.

20

The quirky and unusual

I'VE ALWAYS ENJOYED writing about the more unusual happenings in life...

We all make mistakes and sometimes we try to hide our embarrassment. I must admit to adding to the embarrassment of the *Anglesey Mail* back in 1998 with a brief in several national papers which stated: 'Readers of an Anglesey newspaper have been told that a Spot the Dog competition "has been declared void due to the dog appearing in the photo".'

It was the 'grossest possible provocation' said Judge Huw Daniel when he gave a suspended jail sentence to a 36-year-old Anglesey man who became violent after finding his wife having sex with his own father.

A man of 24 broke into an undertaker's premises and prised open a coffin lid after being told by his brother, a grave digger, that the dead could speak. Solicitor Chris Dawson said in court that his client had explained: 'I started talking to the body and asked him how he felt. I asked him what it was like to be dead.' Added Mr Dawson: 'To his surprise, the body didn't answer.'

There was uproar in the village of Llanelidan, near Ruthin, years ago when the post office and grocery store was closed down when the squire's agent, who ran it, quit. Eventually the GPO provided a mobile post office.

The squire, Sir Vivyan Naylor-Leyland, ex Eton, Oxford and the Grenadier Guards (whose family motto translated is 'Faithful and Audacious'), was riding a magnificent brown horse and wearing a green cloak when he gave me his classy response. 'No comment. I wish we lived in a more civilised day and then I could discuss things with you.' Then he rode away and vanished, as did the store.

Actor Patrick Wymark of *The Power Game* fame on TV, and the traitor in the blockbuster *Where Eagles Dare*, that regular Christmas TV offering, spent a week in 1968 in Colwyn Bay, unpaid, because of his affection for repertory. He produced Noël Coward's *Blithe Spirit* at the Prince of Wales Theatre.

Was he the world's longest commuter? Harland Greenshields travelled between farms at opposite ends of the world – at Caeathro, near Caernarfon, and the Falklands. The cattle farm at Caeathro had 160 acres. The Falklands holding owned by his family for a century comprised 140,000 acres – and 20,000 sheep.

Another long-distance commuter was the Manchester bus conductor who lived in Abergele, 80 miles away, and travelled by train each day.

When the Duke of Edinburgh visited the fisheries experimental station in Conwy, he was instructed about the sex life of an oyster. Later he went on to Anglesey and enjoyed a cold buffet lunch of beef and Scotch salmon. 'We'd been warned he doesn't like oysters,' explained an official.

Maybe it was the 'Londonderry Air', if you'll excuse the pun. After just 17 months stationed there, pre-Troubles, the Royal Welch Fusiliers returned home with 40 Irish wives. 'The figure could rise to 44,' said a battalion spokesman, saying that many of the romances began at a discotheque behind their camp.

After a previous tour in Hong Kong, the lusty soldiers brought home 14 Chinese brides. But not a situation which ensued from their latest deployment – to Afghanistan!

In 1974 the Welsh Language Society demanded that every employee of Gwynedd County Council should be able to speak Welsh. Now they've got their wish and it's even a requirement for a lavatory attendant.

'Captain' (as we dubbed him) Bill Parry's 12,000-mile ambition to sail to Australia in a wartime DUKW ended – with 11,995 miles to go. He set off from Caernarfon but the *Welsh Endeavour*, a veteran of the D-Day landings, was wrecked on Dinas Dinlle beach. Apart from his pride, Bill was unhurt.

Veteran actor Jack Warner, Dixon of Dock Green, was invited to Llandudno police station. Deputy Chief Constable John St David Jones explained: 'We invited him along for a cup of tea and a chat. There is no question that he has done a lot of good for the image of the police.'

The Lord Chancellor, Lord Hailsham, looked into the case of six Welshmen who were given absolute discharges by Bangor magistrates in 1972 for refusing to buy TV licences which weren't in Welsh. The defendants must have been amazed to hear the chairman tell them, in Welsh: 'Gentlemen, I am expressing the unanimous opinion of all the magistrates when I say that it was good for us to be here today. We are grateful to you for your presence.' Although they had broken the law they'd given their reasons 'in a fair and responsible way'. At the end of the case 40 supporters gave the bench a standing ovation.

The magistracy were to provide an even more surprising example of their partiality. Twenty-one Welsh JPs, their names a secret, stumped up cash to enable Dafydd Iwan to be released from prison after he refused to pay £56 in fines and costs following a campaign against English-only road signs.

A honeymooning couple had a disturbed night in their Llandudno hotel room, their intimacy being interrupted by a scraping sound from beneath their bed. Eventually they told their landlady, Jean Barlow, who discovered to her amazement a roosting seagull. So incensed was Mrs Barlow about Llandudno's seagull menace that she penned a letter to the Prime Minister, Edward Health, demanding action.

Road sweeper Hugh Evans, 57, had an entire city to keep tidy. Little wonder that in 1968 councillors in St Asaph wrote to the county council pleading for back-up. One councillor said: 'Mr Evans is very industrious but with the growth of the city it is impossible for one man to cope.' Even so, he managed to sweep every street once a week.

There was no parson, no music and no ceremony at the three-minute funeral in Colwyn Bay crematorium of one of the last century's greatest men, the philosopher Bertrand Russell, 97. Five mourners filed in, observed a silence, then walked out again. Lord Russell, who lived 50 miles away in Penrhyndeudraeth, had requested a secular funeral with no fuss and that's what the former Campaign for Nuclear Disarmament leader got.

There was an unusual crisis in Llanrwst in 1970, caused by the blue and white contraceptive machine in Watling Street outside Henry Walsh's barbershop. Llanrwst urban councillors thought it 'too easily accessible from the street' (though surely that was the whole idea?), so got Denbighshire County Council to draft a special by-law to prohibit it, with the Welsh Secretary, bachelor George Thomas, appending his official signature.

Mr Walsh decided to make other arrangements but observed that 'people in this town are always looking for a sinful side of things. The machine has provided a useful service, particularly on weekend evenings when I've had to refill it.'

Having a good row seems to be endemic among the councillors of Anglesey. Nearly half a century ago, the 68-year-old chairman of Beaumaris Harbour Committee resigned his seat after being called a landlubber by his predecessor, an alderman. William Woods took off his badge of office, a silver oar made in 1723, bowed to the mayor and walked out. 'Being called a landlubber just got my goat,' he protested.

In 1971 members of Deudraeth Rural Council took their responsibilities seriously. Even though they may have been relaxing at home watching TV they would still be 'on duty' – looking out for sex and violence. Any examples 'which go too far' would be brought back to the council, discussed, and if necessary a complaint would be made to the BBC or ITA. 'The morals of some programmes are pretty low,' complained one member.

Mr Justice Mars-Jones, who sometimes presented a fearsome demeanour, reassured a prisoner in the dock in Caernarfon who said he didn't recognise the court. 'Don't worry about that for another second,' he smiled – 'the court recognises you'.

In 1971 Mrs Margery Brownson campaigned against the introduction of fluoride to the water supply in Anglesey where she lived. Each night her husband would return home to Brynsiencyn from work in Bangor (where it wasn't fluoridated) with two gallons of pure water.

The planned South African cricket tour of 1970 was controversial because of apartheid. Student David Wilton-Godberford of Rhos-on-Sea had a cunning plan to disrupt it – by breeding and letting loose thousands of locusts at the grounds to devour the grass. It was a story of mine which went around the world, and the tour never took place. It was called off after pressure from Labour Home Secretary James Callaghan and welcomed by Peter Hain, leader of the anti-apartheid movement. Later that year David, who claimed to be the world's biggest commercial breeder of locusts, sold his business to the Welsh Mountain Zoo. Locusts are apparently a high protein delicacy loved by reptiles, monkeys and even fish.

A boy of three living in Dolwyddelan in the Lledr Valley was so terrified of low-flying jets that he would throw himself to the ground screaming when they passed over his home. The *Daily Express* decided to transport the little lad for a day out at RAF Valley, where he could meet the crews and sit in an aircraft. The Manchester news editor of the *Express* (they had them in those days) dispatched one of his finest reporters for the task. Unfortunately, he drove rather fast and mum and son found the car journey even more stressful than having an RAF jet screaming over their house. Anyway, I received a letter from the clerk of Dolwyddelan Parish Council thanking me for breaking the story.

In 1974 a local builder grabbed the microphone from Michael Foot and tried to drag him from a makeshift platform at Station Square in Colwyn Bay. Unperturbed, the future Labour leader grinned: 'The last time someone tried to drag me off a platform was in Monmouth in 1935. The Tories didn't have very good manners in those days either.'

In Bangor I met a housewife incensed about an injustice caused by the local council. 'I'm going to take them to the OMNIBUS man,' she vowed!

Dwyfor District Council made itself unpopular with ex-servicemen in 1986 when it decided not to allow the band of the Royal Welch Fusiliers to play on its own car park, in keeping with the council ban on the military using any of its facilities. The band played 'We'll Keep a Welcome' as it marched past the gleaming new offices, watched by hundreds and with old sweats walking behind. But perhaps it should have been 'Colonel Bogey'.

A school bus driver, exasperated by the conduct of pupils from Aberconwy School who hurled flour and eggs on his double-decker, exacted his own revenge. But imagine the official fuss after he opened the windows, then drove it through the bus-wash at the Llandudno Junction depot, drenching the children. A union official said: 'Of course he shouldn't have done it but the lads have a lot of sympathy because it wasn't the first time the kids had caused trouble.'

Snowdonia was turned into Scotland when the famous film director Roman Polanski, exiled from the US because of a child sex conviction, filmed *Macbeth*. A thousand hopefuls had turned up in Llan Ffestiniog anxious to be cast as an extra. 'We found that Scotland was ravaged by high tension wires and too far from main routes,' Polanski said when explaining why he chose our mountains.

In the 1980s a magazine suggested, unsuccessfully, that the beautiful Sian Adey-Jones, beauty queen and famous Welsh model, should be made a member of the Gorsedd (order of bards) of the National Eisteddfod, with the title Sian Siapus (Shapely Sian). At the time Welsh-speaking Sian shared her time between Ibiza and Geneva. Her mother Edith wasn't impressed by the idea, nor the title. 'It sounds too much like a racehorse,' she said in Trefnant, near Denbigh.

As early as 1985 the National Eisteddfod was politically correct. At the Rhyl event it was decided, in deference to the anti-apartheid campaign, that in the traditional ceremony to welcome exiles, South Africa would be substituted by 'The Continent of Africa'.

The mystery of a Soviet spy transmitter dug up in 1981 on a farm field at Llanrhaeadr-ym-Mochnant has never been solved. Wrexham MP Tom Ellis wanted to know whether there was a link with a Russian 'trade delegation' which stayed at a smart hotel in the village in 1971. A security expert said: 'It was probably buried in the hope it would never be found – maybe the man operating it feared he was under surveillance.' Somehow, spies and Llanrhaeadr-ym-Mochnant don't belong in the same sentence!

Sometimes the police aren't too clever – like when a senior officer ordered a PC, who had arrived at work smelling of drink, to DRIVE eight miles to Bagillt police station so he could be breathalysed. Sure enough, he was over the limit and was banned. But the breathalyser fiasco was described by his solicitor, John Hughes, with some understatement as 'a matter of some concern'. Unsurprisingly, the police made no comment about this.

A poacher was nabbed in the River Dee, near Bala, not realising that the salmon he caught had a tiny micro-processor in its stomach to study migratory habits.

When farmers get angry they don't indulge in half measures. In 1997, livid about cheap meat imports from Ireland, they stripped an Irish lorry laden with 40 tons of beefburgers at Holyhead port – and hurled them into the sea in their own version of the Boston Tea Party.

An animal-loving couple from Colwyn Bay who went to live on the Costa del Sol hired a taxi to take their rottweiler called Jade and Tigger the tomcat to join them. The bill for the 900-mile journey was nearly £500.

Businessman Andrew Wilford was involved in a long-standing row with North Wales Police, whom he accused of harassing him and stopping his car constantly. On the fourth day of an unsuccessful county court action that he brought, he discovered on his telephone answer machine a conversation between a constable and a Colwyn Bay estate agent. At first, unwisely, the police said in a statement: 'If Mr Wilford has a problem with his phone he should take it up with BT.'

Mr Wilford complained to the Interception of Communications Tribunal. Eventually a top detective from Merseyside was brought in as a neutral outsider to investigate. But even he couldn't be certain what had happened.

Perhaps, if it happened today, it might improve policing and prevent some of those high-profile and sometimes tragic cases of harassment on Britain's council estates. In the village of Newborough, Anglesey, locals had enough of the burglaries and general mayhem caused by a teenager. Two hundred of them marched on his home in 1992 – and subsequently the family had to move out and soon the lout was behind bars.

In 1996 advertising history was made on TV in Wales when ITV and S4C showed, in Welsh and English, a 30-second video extolling a private crematorium near Aberystwyth.

A 'mooner' showed off to his mates in a late-night jape on the main road at Gaerwen in Anglesey, dropping his pants in front of the headlights of an advancing car, forcing it to brake, then running to the pavement. He chose an encore – but this time wasn't quick enough and finished up in hospital with two badly bruised legs after being treated at the scene, his trousers around his ankles. To add insult to injury the 35 year old was told to expect a bill from the driver's insurance company because his bare bottom had smashed the windscreen.

I don't know what the Griffiths Report on national

community care was all about. But it must have been pretty important – because a one-day conference was organised to discuss it. The title: 'Clwyd's Response to the Government's Response to Griffiths.' Bet it was gripping stuff, and that lunch was good, too.

At Abergele court a PC took the oath twice before he gave evidence. The first time, absent-mindedly, he'd been holding a breathalyser instead of a Bible.

Be sure your sins will find you out, as my mother used to say. When a local organist sold tapes of four leading artistes as his own on Llandudno pier he was exposed by an aficionado on holiday. The holidaymaker realised he was hearing the sound of an organ at Blackpool Tower played by John Bowdler. Trading standards officers were called in and the musical cheat got a suspended sentence.

Britain's first full-time radiography Ph.D. student was awarded her doctorate at University of Wales, Bangor, in 1999 – after conducting research on patient anxiety before a barium enema.

In the 1960s a little girl's school report suggested, prophetically, she had 'a masterly hold over mental arithmetic that will prove profitable in later life'. Ysgol y Mair, a Rhyl primary school, had been Carol Vorderman's first. She returned many years later, an established TV star, to inaugurate an internet project.

Annoyed with RAF jets flying so low near his remote cottage near Bala, forestry worker Steve Baughn painted a sign on the roof of his van saying 'P--- off, Biggles.' But pilots changed their flight path just to take a look.

A protester had to pay £135 in a fine and costs after splattering International Development Secretary Clare Short with a custard pie at University of Wales, Bangor. 'As they say, the pie is the great equaliser,' said Claire Hildreth, 34, of Manchester after the case.

21

The biggest fire I ever saw

WHEN THE PHONE rang on a Saturday evening it usually meant that socialising had to be forgotten. However there was the consolation that any work was for the Sunday papers, whose coffers were more generous than those of their daily counterparts.

That day, 23 May 1970, I was nursing a streaming cold and looking forward to an early night. But, at 3 a.m., I was still working and phoning my stories for the late editions.

The blaze which engulfed the Britannia railway bridge which links Anglesey to the mainland, 150ft above the Menai Strait, was so intense that even the steelwork buckled. It took a battalion of firemen hours to put out the flames, and when the still smouldering wreckage was inspected the next day, it was obvious that trains would not pass through again for many, many months.

The immediate story was of a giant investigation to establish whether there could have been sabotage. The answer was much simpler. It was started accidentally by a group of lads in the portals who were searching for bats and set fire to paper to act as a torch. Unfortunately, the flame caught the pitch in the roof of the tubular tunnel – and within minutes there was a conflagration. The centre span on the mainland side was actually sagging. Det. Chief Supt. Anthony Clarke, head of Gwynedd CID, led a team of detectives with the brief to find out who wrecked the masterpiece built by Robert Stephenson in 1850, towering above the swirling, dangerous waters of the Strait. Soon the boys were identified and the mystery solved.

The bridge remained closed for months, and Irish ferry passengers had to be bussed to Bangor across the Menai suspension bridge to catch their connections. George Thomas, Secretary of State for Wales, and local MP Cledwyn Hughes, the Minister of Agriculture, went to survey the damage and were joined by Sir Henry Johnson, chairman of British Rail.

But that burning paper was, in fact, to transform the north Wales transport system. When Stephenson's bridge was reopened an extra deck was installed, providing road traffic with a second link to the island.

Five youngsters appeared at Bangor juvenile court after the fire, a boy of 17 being fined £5 with six guineas costs, and two 15 year olds and two aged 16 having to pay £5 fines and two guineas costs. All five had pleaded guilty to trespassing on the railway.

As Alun Williams declared when prosecuting for British Transport Police: 'Your worships are well aware of the calamitous event which followed this trespass.'

The 17 year old had torn a page from a book and a 15 year old lit it to see if they could spot any bats. Then the first boy had dropped it down the side of a girder. He explained: 'We went for a walk towards the tubular bridge. We jumped on the wall and looked over, then went to where the tunnel opens. We heard what we thought were bats, and after investigating found there were some birds down a girder on the right hand side of the tunnel. It was too dark and we couldn't see. So I found an old book and tore a page. I folded it and another boy lit it. We held it behind a girder but we couldn't see anything. We heard a woman calling and I must have dropped the lighted paper down the back of the girder.'

They walked back to Treborth, then heard someone saying the bridge was on fire. Then they returned and saw the flames at the exact spot where they'd been.

Court chairman O.G. Williams said the bench was

concerned about the lack of security. He said: 'We are here to deal with the offence of trespass and nothing more. We are disturbed by the fact that there has been no reference whatever to security measures which may be in force to guard this vital link in communication.'

I've wondered often whether those five lads, if they've become dads or even granddads, have ever confessed to their children about the night they set alight one of the wonders of Wales, the Britannia bridge.

22

Politics is fun

I'VE ALWAYS BEEN fascinated by politics, and particularly by the humour, the irony, the tricks – and the downright lies.

I never met Winston Churchill but I have covered Clement Attlee, Harold Macmillan, Edward Heath, Harold Wilson, James Callaghan, Lady Thatcher, John Major, Tony Blair, Gordon Brown, David Cameron and Theresa May.

The greatest of them all? For me it has to be Clement Attlee who, though Britain was on its knees after the Second World War (with a deficit worse than we have even now), managed to introduce the NHS.

He was a man of few words, though his 'A period of silence would be welcome' put-down to the troublesome Professor Harold Laski was a classic. Churchill once said Attlee was 'a modest man with much to be modest about,' but later had second thoughts about saying this of the man who soldiered in the trenches of the First World War – he was carried hurt from three battlefields – helped the underprivileged in the East End of London between the wars, and was his faithful No. 2 in the wartime coalition.

When Clement Attlee came to Wellingborough to speak from the back of a lorry in the square during the election of 1955, I looked forward to catching a few words with the great man afterwards to add to the story. 'Have you any message for Wellingborough?' I asked expectantly, after scrambling aboard. 'Yes,' replied Attlee. 'Vote for George – we need him.' And that was it, not a word more. Succinct and to the point you might think, though not what an ambitious young journalist had sought.

He was referring to George Lindgren who clung on to the marginal seat. Attlee's response to heckling by a crowd of boys from Wellingborough School was masterly. He was discussing whether the communist Chinese government should be recognised. 'Like our young friends here we may not like them but we can't pretend they don't exist,' he replied. It's still high in the list of rejoinders I've heard.

Harold Macmillan, 'Super Mac' as they called him, spoke in Belle Vue, Manchester, to an election meeting attended by thousands. I worked on the *News Chronicle* at the time, and it was the Labour *Daily Herald* that was the butt of his laid-back humour. He recalled how they had caricatured him in a cartoon as a bookie when he introduced Premium Bonds, to which the paper was at the time opposed because it would introduce a gambling Britain. Then Mac produced a copy of that day's *Herald* – which was giving away bonds as prizes!

I saw Harold Wilson for the *Daily Mirror* in Bangor on the day that Bill Shankly died. He gave me a quote in tribute, after first explaining, rather pompously I thought, that normally he didn't give off-the-cuff interviews. When his wife Mary spoke in Llandudno she gave a wonderful description of life at No. 10. 'All I know is that we get up early and go to bed late,' she said.

I met James Callaghan in Maentwrog, Snowdonia, in one of his favourite parts of Britain, he said, as he tried to dissuade, vainly, the local electors from defecting from Labour to Plaid Cymru.

Mrs Thatcher, as she was then, I first saw when she spoke at the Welsh Tory conference in Aberystwyth after becoming Leader of the Opposition. Later I interviewed her for radio at the opening of the Pen-y-clip tunnel on the A55. I asked her if she planned to return for the opening of the major tunnel beneath the River Conwy, then under construction. But I don't think she knew anything about it. 'What do you mean?' she asked. Fair enough I suppose, for a Prime Minister who had far more important matters of State to deal with than a north Wales tunnel.

It was during a visit to Llandudno, as Prime Minister, that Mrs Thatcher defined Conservatism in one sentence. 'We set out to enhance the rights and responsibilities of the citizen and to limit the power of the State,' she declared.

Tony Blair gave the impression of being the head of a sleek political machine, which he was. But he was no Attlee! He was a gentleman though, holding open a door for this elderly hack when electioneering in Colwyn Bay!

The greatest speaker I ever heard? That has to be Clement Davies, leader of the Liberals in the post-war years. At the Pier Pavilion, Colwyn Bay, in the 1951 election, he made an impassioned speech praising the Marshall Plan in which the US helped Europe to recover from the war, and left for his next engagement to rapturous applause. Then there was a shout of 'The Candidate' to announce the arrival of the young hopeful for West Denbigh, fresh from a tour of surrounding villages. (There was no TV in those days, and politicians had to meet electors in the flesh.) The candidate's theme? 'It's time we relied more on ourselves and less on the interfering Americans.' The crowd left in confusion. But, as I say, politics is fun. A moral for politicians – always know what the previous speaker has said!

Another tremendous performer was Sir Hartley Shawcross. The former Nuremberg war crimes prosecutor was a Labour government minister who had incurred the wrath of Lord Beaverbrook and had made the famous gaffe in Parliament 'We are the masters now'. So when he spoke in Old Colwyn I was asked by the *Daily Express* to provide a verbatim report of anything he said about the paper. In the event, it was nothing.

When Denis Healey (who I also interviewed for radio) spoke in Bangor, he introduced a note of religion with a reference to 'My Brother's Keeper'. But you would bring religion into a talk at chapel-going Bangor (as it was then), wouldn't you?

The most choleric politician I ever met was George Brown, at one time Labour Deputy Prime Minister. The first occasion was when, on the *Daily Herald*, I was sent to Dewsbury one Sunday to try and downplay his most recent faux pas featured in a Tory paper.

However, it was in Conwy, supporting the party's MP Ednyfed Hudson Davies (apparently later known in south Wales as 'Labour's Eddie Davies') that George really put his foot in it. Poor Ednyfed had the slimmest majority in Wales and suffered one of the most frustrating days of his political life.

First, because it was raining in Conwy, George withdrew to the Liverpool Arms on the riverside, buttonholed an attractive student, and loudly composed 'An Ode to Cheryl'. It made page one of the *Sun*.

Far worse was to come when George reached Bangor – and this was at a time when nationalism and the fight for the Welsh language were getting stronger by the day. Heckled by a nationalist, George replied: 'I'm a Celt, an Irish boyo, and I recognise a little better than you do that what matters is what the little lady spends in the butcher's shop, rather more than the bloody language.'

Predictably, Plaid Cymru asked Ednyfed Hudson Davies to disassociate himself from such blasphemous remarks. And equally predictably, Peter Thomas won the seat for the Tories. Elwyn Roberts, national secretary of Plaid Cymru, said: 'We consider that Mr Brown has put many thousands of votes in our hands.' Not quite. George Brown was the first and only politician to refer to the language of heaven, at least publicly, as 'the bloody language'.

One of the greatest intellects I encountered (and interviewed on radio) was Enoch Powell, the Greek scholar who could speak in perfect academic Welsh. It is a tragedy that his notorious and ill-judged 'Rivers of Blood' speech is for what he is most remembered. He had in my view one of the most brilliant minds in post-war politics.

What about this for a speech – the one he made to Conservatives in Prestatyn in 1968, which some may feel is as apposite today as it was then?

Mr Powell said that if it was the real desire of Wales and Scotland 'to be a nation' it should not be resisted. But he added a caveat...

He threw down the gauntlet to nationalists by saying that self-government would have to mean complete self-government, like the Irish Republic.

'Conservatives – the nationalists par excellence – cannot just be silent,' he declared. He devoted his entire speech to what he called 'perhaps the most serious of all political subjects, the unity of the kingdom'.

Mr Powell said if it were ever the preponderant and settled wish of Wales or Scotland 'to be themselves a nation and therefore no longer to be part of this nation, that ought not to be resisted.

'But we must be clear and firm about what being a nation in this context means. It does not mean enjoying independence at other people's expense.

'It does not mean having the best of both worlds, the penny of one's own nationhood and the biscuit of being part of a large and wealthy nation.

'If the thing is not to be a mockery and an insult to the pride and intelligence of those concerned, it means having all the essentials of sovereignty – government, currency, central bank, parliament, taxation, laws, police, defence.

'It means being approximately as the Republic of Ireland is today.

'If that is to be the decision, it must be taken in full light of day and taken as a single deliberate, responsible, once-for-all decision.'

He said that until such a decision was taken no institution should be created in Wales or Scotland which implied acceptance of the thesis of separate nationhood.

'Unless and until the great decision has been faced and

taken, Great Britain must be governed and administered as one nation. If ever it was felt right for Wales or Scotland to be represented in a separate and exclusive parliament, then it would be a declaration that one nation no longer existed.'

Mr Powell had gone beyond party policy. What he was saying to the nationalists was that if there were to be self-government it would have to be complete – with no convenient half measures. What a wonderful expression – 'the penny and the biscuit'.

Listen to what the late Wyn Roberts, the then Minister for Wales, said in 1994: 'Labour's case for a Welsh Assembly is motivated by a crazy lust for power.' Labour wanted to increase its stranglehold on Wales 'and this would be a recipe for unfairness, division and conflict'.

Now even the Tories support devolution. But some, particularly in the neglected north, still think that what Wyn said was spot-on.

I always had a great deal of time for Wyn Roberts who became Lord Roberts of Conwy before his death in December 2013. For a record 15 years until 1994 he was a Welsh Office minister.

Wyn piloted the Welsh Language Act of 1983 and this son of the manse – his brother Eifion became an eminent QC and judge – is credited with doing more for the Welsh language than any man alive. With good humour he endured years of hostility from language zealots, who once even 'imprisoned' him in his constituency office in Bangor. (Eifion, incidentally, I once heard deliver a brilliant 20-minute judgment in a county court case without reading from a note.)

In 1996 Wyn called it 'a very sad day' when 'zealots and fanatics' forced the Queen to curtail her first visit to Aberystwyth in 41 years. Rod Richards MP, then a Welsh Office minister, went further and urged the university to throw them out. (It was Rod Richards who described Welsh Labour councillors as 'short, fat, slimy and fundamentally corrupt'. It provoked outrage, as expected, but he explained that it was tongue-in-cheek, no offence was intended 'and many of them are charming people'.)

When police in Aberystwyth decided it was wiser that the Queen did not open the Centre for Glaciology, those students succeeded where even the IRA had failed – by forcing her to leave early. College Vice-Chancellor, Professor Derec Llwyd Morgan, accused the police of not acting 'stoutly enough' to defend the head of state; many townspeople, including the mayor, said the name of Aberystwyth had been tarnished.

According to Dyfed Powys Police, the Queen's safety and dignity could not be assured, and the decision to cut short her visit was taken for sound reasons 'with great reluctance'. Chief Constable Raymond White explained that many protesters had assembled on high ground, 'were in an aggressive mood and eggs were found, indicating an intention that egg and other missile throwing was likely to take place'. Locals wondered whether she would ever come again. I stand to be corrected but I don't think she has returned.

I was at St Thomas' Church, Rhyl, for a special service for Sir Anthony Meyer to mark his services to the locality. One of the lessons was read by the Welsh nationalist Dafydd Elis-Thomas. Funny thing, politics. But of course both men were rebels at heart.

In the 1980s Sir Anthony had wrested the Tory nomination as Parliamentary candidate from Beata Brookes in a 'night of the long knives' in the Kinmel Manor Hotel in Abergele. In the same hotel a few years later there was another bitter drama when Sir Anthony was deselected after having put himself forward as the 'stalking horse' against Mrs Thatcher – to be succeeded by Rod Richards, whose political career was later to end on a sombre note.

Labour's John Prescott – now Lord – is the son of a Prestatyn railway signalman. 'Our relationship with the trade unions and Clause IV is as relevant today as ever,' he declared in 1992 in Llandudno. Clause IV historically set out the aims and values of the party. And he hit out at 'red roses, pretty faces and jazzy

146

TV presentations'. Yet it was that combination which won the 1997 election – when any talk of Clause IV was banished.

Of course his claim to fame in north Wales will always be 'the Prescott punch', the night he hit back when Craig Evans, a 29-year-old farm worker, hurled an egg. Ludicrously, North Wales Police spent £9,000 on the inquiry, during which detectives went to see Prescott at his Hull constituency. The file was sent to a special unit of the CPS in York. North Wales Police announced weeks later: 'The CPS has conducted a careful review of the substantial file of evidence and video material presented by investigators. The conclusion in Mr Prescott's case is that, for reasons of self-defence, there is not a realistic prospect of a conviction.

'In Mr Evans's case, the CPS has concluded that a prosecution would serve no useful purpose, taking into account the minor nature of the assault, as well as the fact that he suffered some minor injury himself and spent several hours in police custody. Neither party has made any allegations about this incident. Accordingly, no further police action is anticipated.'

One can only wonder why it took four months and £9,000! When officials spend our cash in that way is it any wonder that the country's finances are diminished? Before the 2010 general election, John Prescott returned to Rhyl and was helpfully provided with a boxing glove at the same spot outside the Little Theatre so that the episode could be re-enacted and, of course, photographed.

The most hopeless prophesy I ever heard? That was in Llandudno at the former Odeon theatre in 1981 when David Steel declared: 'I have the good fortune to be the first Liberal leader for over half a century who is able to say "go back to your constituencies and prepare for government".' He was 29 years too early.

I like to call politicians of all parties my friends, and that includes Plaid Cymru. But some of Plaid's allies worry me, though possibly younger adherents have acted more from naivety than conviction. I hope so, because one day, in the Conwy Valley, I watched enthusiastic members of the Welsh Language Society daub holiday homes owned by English families with green paint and fill the locks with glue. To me, this had too many similarities with historic and notorious events abroad.

23

Among those I have met

FOR RADIO I interviewed the gracious and charming Lady Olwen Carey Evans, then the only surviving child of Lloyd George. At the age of 93 and still driving her car into Criccieth daily, she'd written her autobiography – 'to set the record straight', as she explained.

She said the family had been upset by the habit of historians, writers and TV producers to place too great an emphasis on 'father's little peccadilloes'.

Lady Olwen said: 'The book is the true story of our lives; so much junk has been written about my father and mother. It's only a simple book written by a simple old lady. I had a very extraordinary father who wasn't like any other father. He was a family man, whether in No. 10 in the First World War or back home in Wales.'

Discussing his infidelity, she said she was aware from an early age that there were other women in his life. 'Most of his affairs were little more than amorous adventures adding excitement to his life of work,' she believed. She criticised the modern fashion 'to debase and debunk' the great men of the past, from whatever background.

'Father was sweet and kind, Mother was adorable and we couldn't have had a happier time,' she told me. Lloyd George's grandson, David Carey Evans, spoke at the Colwyn Bay Civic Society and said that the Prime Minister's greatest achievement was the introduction of the old age pension. How right. I can still hear my nain (grandmother), poor all her life, announce on a Friday: 'I'm off to the Post Office to collect my Lloyd George.' His pensions saved millions from penury.

Another impressive woman was Mary Winch who suffered grievous injustices from the legal and medical system which could have made the plot for a Dickens novel.

I first met her when I was phoned by a friend of Mary's, incensed because she'd been sectioned and put in a mental hospital – on the say-so, he said, of a doctor on a darkened veranda at the entrance to the establishment. In 1996 she accepted an out-of-court settlement after suing the Home Office, her doctors and lawyers – and, typically, leaving the money to cancer research, child and animal charities.

Mary was once a senior secretary at University College of North Wales, Bangor, and also secretary to the Lord Lieutenant of Caernarfonshire. A judge jailed her for contempt of court when she refused to part with documents relating to her mother's estate, and she spent three months in Risley, near Warrington – 'Grisly Risley' as it was called because of its dreadful reputation. When prison doctors heard her list of complaints against lawyers, they concluded she was mad and she had to suffer a year locked up in the North Wales Hospital in Denbigh.

Mary wasn't mad – but gentle and clever. Eventually she found good friends, some in the legal profession, and was vindicated.

Sometimes, even I get disillusioned by the failings of modern journalism. But then I read Mary Winch's words which make me proud to be a member of the profession: 'Until people saw my case featured in the paper, nobody knew the truth.'

She also said: 'The law is too important to be left to the lawyers. Yet there are times when, as happened in my case, they literally hold your life in their hands.'

Roger Roberts, now Lord Roberts of Llandudno, who campaigned valiantly for her alongside Liberal MP Simon Hughes, said: 'I think this case is as important for the civil law as that of the Birmingham Six was for the criminal law. It's a condemnation of our legal system that an innocent citizen should be forced to suffer 20 years of harassment, imprisonment and homelessness.'

And, as he put it: 'How many others are suffering in similar ways? That's the most frightening question of all.'

Another remarkable character was Bob Walton, who was so angry when youngsters stole his war medals that he put up his Snowdonia cottage for sale. It was a sad story because Bob used his home at Rachub as a base from which he explored the mountains. 'The medals mean everything to me but are worthless to anyone else,' he said.

What a war record! He fought at Dunkirk and, as a colour sergeant in the Parachute Regiment, he was one of those who parachuted into France hours before the main D-Day invasion force. 'I remember it clearly, I landed smoking my pipe, as I always did,' he recalled.

Later in the European campaign he was commissioned in the field by the legendary General Gale. 'I can still hear him ordering me to take that so-and-so crown off my sleeve and put it on my shoulder.' Once, Bob's life was saved when a bullet struck his mess tin. But he believed he got his revenge by shooting Rommel with an anti-tank weapon. 'I was in a wood in France and took aim at this German staff car. Afterwards I was told that Rommel had been hit up the backside by the blast and injured.'

The theft of Bob's medals caused great anger. And his MP, Wyn Roberts, and the British Legion promised to help in finding him somewhere safer to live. Safer than Rachub? What had we come to?

It was in Snowdonia in 1973 that I met some of the most famous men in the world when 60 climbers arrived to celebrate the 20th anniversary of the conquering of Everest. They stopped at the Pen-y-Gwryd Hotel, headquarters when training for the 1953 expedition, and, fittingly, 20 of them climbed a 3,000ft peak in the Carneddau. Sir Edmund Hillary couldn't be there because his wife had had an accident back home in New Zealand. But the leader, Lord Hunt, was present, as was Sherpa Tenzing who had stood on the summit with Hillary.

A less taxing Snowdonia stroll was taken by 82-year-old Professor Noel Odell who had been the last person to see Irvine and Mallory alive at 28,000ft in their epic but tragic Everest attempt of 1924.

24

Truly greats

ARTHUR ROWLANDS, BLINDED policeman and George
Medallist, was one of the finest men I ever met. Blinded
by a mad gunman, Arthur showed not a trace of bitterness
nor ill-will but a humour and generosity of spirit that was
inspiring.

Many years ago, when he was working on the specially
adapted switchboard at Caernarfon police headquarters,
he told me one morning: 'I was kissed by a lovely lady last
night.' It was the embrace of my mother, always soft-hearted
and kind, who had been touched when he spoke to a meeting
at Bethlehem Chapel, Colwyn Bay, and had thanked him
afterwards.

In 1961 he was shot with a sawn-off shotgun by Robert
Boynton, who was later judged criminally insane and locked
up in Broadmoor where he died in 1994. It happened on the
banks of the river, yards from Dovey Bridge on the outskirts of
Machynlleth in wonderful countryside. Arthur's life sentence
of darkness had been met with stoicism, and he held important
positions with the Society for the Blind and The Guide Dogs for
the Blind Association, lecturing in schools and broadcasting.
He was also a chapel deacon, and told me that Christianity was
the key to his life.

In a remarkable interview Arthur recalled to me how in the
early days after fighting for his life at St Lawrence Hospital,
Bristol, he felt despair and even bitterness. Then a visiting
police constable took him on a tour of some of the other wards.

'I heard the cries of young children and my friend said "I'm glad you can't see the kids, Arthur".

'It was the ward where Thalidomide children were being looked after. That was the turning point for me,' he revealed.

'I've no bitterness towards Robert Boynton – after all, he's a fellow human being.' Arthur said it was because of his Christian beliefs and the selflessness of his family that he had dealt so successfully with blindness. 'My mother used to tell me that if you can help someone you will be paid in heaven,' he said. 'I have always believed that to be a wonderful philosophy.' What a remarkable, wonderful man! He died, aged 90, in December 2012. I was at his funeral, not surprisingly in a packed chapel in Caernarfon.

Another great man bestowed with the same standards was Gwynn Davies. I knew him first as a solicitor with the then Caernarfonshire County Council, and later as the clerk to Llandudno magistrates. Gwynn, who had a great sense of humour, rang me one day from court. 'Mr Bellis [he always called me that], you must come today,' he said. It was a theft that really tickled Gwynn, and it also achieved great publicity. An Irishman, walking along Mostyn Street in Llandudno, decided to steal a pair of shoes – and was caught running down the street wearing two right-footed ones. Magistrates treated him sympathetically, even after he tried to convince them: 'I bought the shoes in Dublin.'

It was the gift that he bestowed on the handicapped that is Gwynn's greatest memorial. He founded Antur Waunfawr, near Caernarfon, where Down's sufferers and others are able to work in a market garden, shops and a café. (In my family Down's has a special meaning, because of our grandchild Charlotte.) Gwynn gave up his job so that he could devote his time exclusively to this wonderful venture in the hills. I mentioned to a friend of his that it was strange that Gwynn had never received a decoration to mark 30 years of wonderful work. 'Maybe he wouldn't accept a medal,' was the response. I wonder?

A persuasive voice for the handicapped, he also established personal 'advocates' to work on behalf of mental patients. If ever a man left the world a better place than he found it, Gwynn Davies was the name.

I never had the privilege to meet Leonard Cheshire VC, the great wartime hero who was to start those wonderful Cheshire Homes, including one in Colwyn Bay. When the north Wales branch of the Aircrew Association wrote to him sympathising about his illness three weeks before his death from motor neurone disease in 1992, they received a wonderful and inspiring reply from his secretary, who said the disease was progressing quicker than expected.

'However, he's meeting the situation with characteristic courage and faith and is in good heart. To use an RAF expression, he refers to his illness as a little bit of flak on the way to the target.'

Frank Jones of Llandudno, a flight engineer on Handley Page Halifax bombers and secretary of the north Wales branch, could recall the voice of Leonard Cheshire, the 'master bomber', approaching the target. 'Go in lads,' he'd say.

'A little bit of flak on the way to the target' could be the theme for a sermon! What a great man. Recently I visited a National Trust mansion in Yorkshire where bomber crews, including Cheshire's, were based. Vacant beds became the norm, crews facing less of a chance of survival than men in the trenches in the First World War.

I met some more great men when I attended the granting of a new standard for the north Wales branch of the Russian Convoy Club. These are the men who braved those bitter seas as they delivered some of the arms which helped Stalin in the Second World War.

The Marble Church in Bodelwyddan was a fitting venue for the ceremony. The standard was carried by Geoffrey Bye of Rhyl who served on the battleship *King George V*. Also there was Walter Jones of Prestatyn who, as a teenager – yes, a teenager! – survived after the destroyer *Punjabi* was split in two by the *King George V* in thick fog in one of the greatest tragedies of the war. He described how some of his shipmates were killed by the cold and others by depth charges which rolled off the destroyer and exploded. Those heroes in their white berets are still to be seen at Remembrance Day ceremonies, although their numbers are fast dwindling.

Many of my heroes were from the Second World War. Lord Newborough was a peer with a wonderful war record and a zest for mischief who left the world with a bang in 1998. His ashes were fired from an antique cannon on his estate at Rhug, near Corwen, into trees known as The Big Wood after hundreds of his friends had attended a memorial service – with bright ties the order of the day for men. After a champagne reception the 81-year-old peer's son, the new Lord Newborough, Robert Wynn, lit the fuse. In red regalia, retired hunt master Robin Gundry sounded 'Gone Away' on his horn and there were three cheers as an era ended in style, as meticulously planned by the departed Lord Newborough.

He died on holiday in Turkey and had a war record which was the stuff of *Boy's Own* – invalided out of the army, sailing five times into Dunkirk as a civilian to take troops off the beaches, then obtaining a naval commission and in 1942 being awarded the DSC after being shot off the bridge of his motor torpedo boat in the famous but costly commando raid on St Nazaire. It was he who was involved in the plan to fill HMS *Campbeltown* with explosives, then sink it to block the harbour, an operation which became an acclaimed film. Being one of the awkward squad as far as his German captors were concerned, he inevitably ended up in Colditz – then was repatriated after feigning madness.

Sir Donald Wilson, a Cheshire farmer and close friend, said at the ashes ceremony: 'What a wonderful character – there will never be another Micky Wynn.' And about the Colditz repatriation, he grinned: 'I suspect we lost a great actor on the British stage.'

In 1976 the impish Lord Newborough had been fined £25

for sending a cannonball through the mast of a yacht as it sailed on the Menai Strait, fired from a battery of antique guns at his former estate, Fort Belan, near Caernarfon. In court he explained it was a salute to mark his mother-in-law's birthday. The cannonball incident wasn't his first. It emerged several years later that in 1969, on the eve of the Investiture, one had landed near the yacht of Lord Snowdon who was taking guests to a cocktail party at Fort Belan. What a character!

A more peaceful personality whom I had the privilege to meet was Mrs Leonora Cohen, Britain's oldest surviving suffragette, who reached the age of 101. She had been the 'official bodyguard' to Mrs Pankhurst.

It was hard to believe that this quiet, dignified and unassuming old lady whom I met in a retirement home for vegetarians in Rhos-on-Sea, had once been placed in a dungeon at the Tower of London to await the police after smashing a glass case in the Jewel House in one of the most spectacular protests of the suffragette era.

Just before her 100th birthday she told me: 'Memories come flooding back and I remember one birthday which I spent in a lock-up after being arrested. Nowadays there are marvellous opportunities for women, unlike in my young days when everything was under the influence of masculine supremacy.'

For 93 years of her life Mrs Cohen lived in Leeds where she was a JP for 30 years, and in 1928 she was appointed OBE for her social work. At 100, there was one feature of modern life which appalled her – the abuse of abortion. Her belief was that it should be allowed only if a life was at stake. 'I believe in freedom – but not licence,' she declared.

How much more noble were her protests as a suffragette than the firebomb plotters of Wales who cared not who could have been maimed, disfigured or killed during their law-breaking campaign, and who were never arrested!

25

Those with smiling faces

SOMETIMES YOU BECOME tired of writing about wickedness and unhappiness and it is pleasant to come across the other side of the coin – like a traffic warden in Ruthin called Mrs Mary Jones.

In the summer of 1972, 33 old people, the oldest aged 93, arrived by coach in the town on a blazing day. As soon as it pulled up in The Square there was Mrs Jones, not like her modern-day equivalent with a notebook and incriminating camera at the ready, but with words and deeds of kindness.

She helped them to get off the coach, found seats on The Square for some of the invalids, and asked local people to move up and make more room. Mrs Jones even escorted one invalid to a shop where she could buy a Welsh hat – and paid for it herself. When an elderly man wandered off, she found him and brought him back.

'Her kindness to the old people was out of this world,' said the secretary of the League of Friends, from Birkenhead, who had organised the trip. 'She even gave up some of her time off to help us, and see that everyone got back on the coach in safety.'

The League wrote to the police, then in charge of traffic wardens, to express their thanks. 'It's not the first time people have praised Mrs Jones,' said Inspector John Hughes.

Mrs Jones, unlike some of today's jobsworth counterparts who have the sinister official title of 'enforcement officers', would never need to be sent on a 'customer care course'.

A smiling face was lost to Llandudno in 1986 with the death of comedian Alex Munro, who for 20 years ran an open-air show in the Happy Valley at the foot of the Great Orme headland. Those who paid sat in deckchairs, those who didn't stood at the back on what the Scots comic called 'Aberdeen Hill'. Nothing could deter Alex, not even a rainy day.

His posters proclaimed: IWTH ('If Wet – Town Hall'). As the vicar said at his funeral: 'When God created Alex he gave him a twinkle in his eye.'

I saw smiling faces, too – of hope and expectancy – one night in October 1972. I had driven nearly 70 miles to Tonfanau camp, west of Dolgellau, familiar to thousands of ex-servicemen who had served there with the Royal Artillery.

The camp had been closed down and was chosen as an ideal location to house hundreds of Ugandan refugees who had fled their own country. They arrived by train and one little boy popped his head out of a carriage window and asked: 'Is this Wales?'

Altogether, 1,580 were given a welcome in the hillsides of Merioneth, and most of them had barely a penny to call their own. By the following April the last hundred had left to new homes.

The Ugandans were noted for their work ethic, and within a few years some were to become millionaires in their adopted country – of England. If only some had stayed in Merioneth! I wonder what happened to that cheerful little boy?

26

Famous funerals

YOU WOULDN'T EXPECT to find two of the world's most famous people in Llanfihangel-y-traethau in Gwynedd, listening to the sound of Welsh hymn singing.

Yet in 1985 that was the scene at the little churchyard near Talsarnau where Senator Edward Kennedy and Jackie Onassis stood together.

The occasion was the funeral of Lord Harlech, one-time ambassador in Washington and close friend of President Kennedy, and also, it's been revealed recently, the one-time suitor of Jackie who had turned him down. The pair stepped forward at the end of the ceremony to give the Sign of the Cross alongside the grave, Mrs Onassis near to tears. I wonder what was going through her mind? Also there were the Senator's sister Mrs Jean Smith and his 21-year-old nephew Mark Shriver.

Apart from Lord Harlech's heavily veiled widow, Pamela, other distinguished mourners were the Duke and Duchess of Devonshire, Roy Jenkins and his wife, and Lord and Lady Anglesey.

An address at the 12th-century church was given by the Rev. Robert Hughes of Birmingham, a close friend of Lord Harlech, and son of the novelist Richard Hughes.

'He will share this place with farmers who have worked these hills for generations, who have never travelled further than the markets of Dolgellau or Caernarfon,' he told the congregation.

'He will share it too with sea captains – sea captains who are at home on every continent and masters of every sea in the world.'

A circular wreath of green and yellow orchids and white cyclamen bore the inscription: 'With much love, the Kennedy family.'

Senator Kennedy issued his own written tribute: 'David was Jack's best friend in Britain,' he said. The original version said 'in England'. Then a reporter diplomatically pointed out that this was Wales – and the change was made. It was fitting that the reporter, I recall, was from Harlech TV.

I was at another remarkable funeral not far away – in Porthmadog. It was in 1991 of the 84-year-old rags-to-riches local boy Jack Evans, who made a fortune from oil in the USA. He died on a business trip to Mexico and his ashes were returned to Porthmadog to be interred in his mother's grave.

Jack had been described as the personification of the American dream, orphaned at ten, going to sea at 14, emigrating to Canada at 17 with just £1 in his pocket, entering the US as an illegal immigrant, once working in a speakeasy, joining the US Air Force as a private during the Second World War and leaving as a full colonel, then starting in business on his own and making his millions.

His second cousin, Dafydd Davies of Porthmadog, predicted: 'It's going to be some funeral. But then Jack was some man, believe me.'

Three hundred relatives and friends were there. A funeral march through the town passed his former home – led by the world-famous black jazzmen flown in from New Orleans, Milton Batiste's Olympia Brass Band. They were known to millions for their part in the Bond film *Live and Let Die*.

Porthmadog had never seen a funeral like it. Just a pity it had to rain!

Then there was the funeral of Louis Parker, the showbiz starmaker who first made his name when he ran a nightclub in St Asaph which made nationwide headlines with its stunts – such as the record number of people inside a telephone box or a Mini – some very funny, others outrageous.

He was only 49 when he died from cancer and 700 packed St Asaph Cathedral for the service, including the pop group Boyzone. Before the coffin was carried through the door after the service, the congregation broke into spontaneous applause – similar to that at the funeral of Princess Diana and perhaps the first time it had happened in the cathedral's 700 years.

The hearse was escorted by police and Hells Angels. Louis was the head of an international showbiz and tour management company in London and helped to promote many famous pop groups.

A musician from the Central Band of the Royal Air Force performed the 'Last Post' in Bangor Cathedral at the funeral of a friend of mine, 91-year-old Max Aiken, in 2001, an unassuming war hero I'd known for 30 years, ever since he saved the Grand Hotel in Llandudno from ruin. Even at the age of 91, shortly before he died of cancer, Max had been turning up for work at the British Hotel, Bangor, owned by him and wife Pat. Max, with David Niven looks, appeared on page one of the *Daily Express* during the Second World War with other pilots meeting King George VI. He had once piloted General de Gaulle, the Free French leader, as well as other VIPs and even German generals who'd been captured. He also ferried agents to and from occupied France. So when a bearer party from RAF Valley carried the coffin, draped in the Union flag, it was no more than Max, the master hotelier and brave flier, deserved.

27

A little night music – and police generosity

I'VE ALWAYS SUPPORTED and had a great deal to do with the police, even writing the North Wales Police handbook some years ago. In recent years, however, there's been a change, much of it to do with the national culture – but a significant amount to do with police chiefs too happy to adopt the modern strangulating curse of political correctness and targets, abandoning the human face of policing.

It was certainly not the case in 1969 when PC Huw Williams, the 'Singing Policeman', came across 45 unhappy pensioners stranded in a coach which was too wide to negotiate a narrow lane near Eglwysbach in the Conwy Valley. This was before the days of Satnav!

In a rich bass voice which had achieved Eisteddfod successes, the 39-year-old PC knew exactly how to cheer up the pensioners. He struck up 'The Bold Gendarmes', and his captive audience joined in the 'We'll Run Them In' chorus.

Then he chose another from his repertoire, the very apt 'If I Can Help Somebody', by which time the pensioners were recovering their spirits and joined in a sing-song.

After a few hours all the pensioners were back in their Llandudno hotel, three diabetics in their 80s and a woman of 92 being taken by PC Williams in his own car.

They were from a club in Bramhall, Cheshire, and they wrote

a letter of appreciation to the Chief Constable, Lieutenant Colonel Jones-Williams. Organiser Mrs Jessie Boardman said: 'PC Williams made everyone feel happy and put them all in a different frame of mind. When he picked up the four in the car he sang to them on the way back to Llandudno.

'We just cannot forget him. And we are also grateful for the kindness of a farmer's wife who brought us pots of tea and bread-and-butter.'

PC Williams said: 'I only sang to them to keep up their spirits. If you can take their minds off something it is always the best thing to do.'

If my memory is correct the story was a page lead in the *Sunday Express*. I wonder if 'We'll Keep a Welcome' was in his repertoire that night? It should have been.

Here's another story which shows a human side of the police in the old days. When 20-year-old Canadian tourist Joan Swinford left hospital after three days, having fallen 150ft on the Great Orme in Llandudno, a police car was waiting to whisk her to 'the nick'. There she was presented with a basket of fruit, a bouquet of tulips and a framed photograph of the Orme, after bobbies held a whip-round. A senior officer explained: 'This young lady is 3,000 miles from home and on her own. We thought what it would be like for our own children if they had a similar mishap far away, and wanted to cheer her up.' This was in 1972, and in another age.

Would it happen today? I doubt it. In those days police had the time to think about the important side of their job, relating with the public.

Such gestures make a Press Office redundant. Good deeds don't need spin because word spreads. And just as important, they don't cost anything and spread a little happiness.

28

Law and order

WHEN I WAS a lad of 17 I called at Colwyn Bay police station on my way to work each day on behalf of the *Pioneer* to ask: 'Anything doing?' Usually I was assured, mostly truthfully: 'All quiet on the Western Front.'

In north Wales and other places where I've worked, particularly in Manchester and Liverpool, crime stories were written because there was mutual trust. I've received letters thanking me for help and support. But not any more!

I suppose the Blair government, with its emphasis on spin and targets, started it all. More recently the Leveson Inquiry has encouraged the idea that the Press is no longer the natural conduit between police and public. The fact that an officer has to make an official note if he speaks to a journalist has the obvious effect of discouraging any interplay.

When I sought, through a Freedom of Information request, to ask North Wales Police if officers had to note any contact with other professions and trades, such as lawyers, accountants and scrap metal dealers, the answer was 'No'. Even a senior officer, when talking to journalists, is expected to have a Press Officer at his side, as if he or she, or the journalist, cannot be trusted.

In North Wales Chief Constable Richard Brunstrom had a controversial nine-year reign, with 'initiatives' including officers in T-shirts and baseball caps and a 'mounted section' of four horses, later abolished because of the cost. But he was an ideas man who never sought to hide and probably, at the time, was the best-known chief constable in Britain, mostly because of the activities of journalists and even photographers. He became proficient in the Welsh language in record time, putting many of us to shame.

Recent years have seen the scrapping of police authorities, to be replaced, controversially, by politically elected Police and Crime Commissioners. Serving on a police authority was a nice little earner – it was my great friend, the late Ivor Wynne Jones, columnist on the *Daily Post*, who once revealed that these important people were paid 'reading time' for poring over their documents at home.

I got on well with most chief constables, including David Owen and the urbane Sir Philip Myers whose funeral I attended. St Paul's in Colwyn Bay was packed to the doors – which said it all.

When David Owen retired in 1994 after 12 years as head of the force and 42 as a bobby, he spoke of his fear that policing would become more centralised, directed by a 'Minister of the Interior'. He said: 'That would be the end of the British policing system. What we need to remember is that it is cherished by us in Britain and is the envy of the world.' His funeral in Llandudno recently also saw a packed church for a chief who was born at the police station in Betws-y-Coed where his father was the sergeant.

Well, his fear has almost materialised. To be fair, I suppose Mrs Thatcher played a sinister part in this, with police being used as her personal army in the miners' strike, freedom of movement being curtailed with no legal basis.

What was to follow from a Labour government was far worse, a police service hidebound by paperwork and targets from the Home Office, sometimes more to do with social engineering than with crime fighting. Then there was the ridiculous situation when North Wales Police detectives were sent to London after Anne Robinson was adjudged to have made a TV comment about the Welsh which could be racially insensitive. The emblem of Stonewall appeared on police notepaper, the flag of Gay Pride flew from outside police headquarters. Why should certain groups be given preferential treatment and others left out?

To quote David Owen once again: 'I'm very concerned that a large number of people who are not thinking, are not consulting, are following a dogma of their political agendas and they're going to take us down the road of the destruction of the British police service.'

In 1973 the then Home Secretary, Robert Carr, unveiled a mural crafted by one of the country's leading sculptors, Jonah Jones, entitled 'Peace over Gwynedd', in the foyer of police headquarters in Colwyn Bay. Less than 30 years later, to the horror of many, the slate and marble work of art was ripped from the wall and dumped in a skip during refurbishment work. It was claimed by the police authority that it would not be possible to reassemble it.

'It's a philistine thing to do,' was the reaction of 83-year-old Jonah Jones when I broke the news to him. 'You would have thought they might have told me.' They didn't even have the courtesy to tell the creator that his sculpture was being destroyed. Perhaps they were too ashamed.

Of all the quangos and semi-quangos I've known, the North Wales Police Authority was near the bottom of the list in my regard, close to the media-unfriendly Education Workforce Council. There were one or two members on the Authority cleverer than the rest who were prepared to speak their minds. One prominent member claimed, in all seriousness, that the public WANTED to pay five per cent more for their police.

I'm an unashamed believer in individual liberty. Our lives should not be blighted by unnecessary laws (more than 4,000 new regulations from the Blair government). The new breed of 'civil enforcement officers', aided by thousands of cameras, worries me. I'm opposed to smoking but don't think those who indulge should be criminalised to the extent they are, like a lorry driver having to pay hundreds of pounds in court for lighting up in the cab during his lunch break. Drop a piece

167

of paper accidentally and a black-clad, camera-wearing 'civil enforcement officer' will pounce, though after many protests the firm that provided them is no longer active in north Wales. Conwy Council said the departure meant a huge loss of fines revenue – which says it all.

What about the administration of justice itself? Gone are the days when the local squire was the chairman of the magistrates' bench. But now the court system has been hit by cuts which not only affect legal practitioners and the court infrastructure, but, most importantly, defendants and witnesses. Often hearings are delayed for as long as 18 months due to overworked CPS staff or police problems. Barristers and solicitors have told me that because of legal aid reductions, fees have been reduced to such an extent that the substantial payments of the past are but a distant memory. Other cost cutting measures have meant that in north Wales the number of magistrates' courts has been reduced so drastically that defendants and witnesses often have to travel many miles to get a hearing. Tywyn to Caernarfon, for instance, can be a tortuous journey for those without a car, as can Corwen to Llandudno. The biggest victims of all, of course, are the ordinary people – witnesses and defendants. With there no longer a court in Prestatyn, they are forced to travel to Llandudno. Small wonder that hearings often continue into the evening – a situation which would not be allowed in the crown court. Perhaps Chris Grayling ('Failing Grayling'), the former justice secretary, should come and look at some of his handiwork!

29

A very personal mystery

SOMETIMES YOU HAVE to write about someone you know very well. Such was the case when Emrys Woodfine, 64, vanished in early 1991 – and has never been seen since.

His unlocked car was found, apparently abandoned, near the Little Orme headland at Penrhyn Bay. The massive cliff faces and beaches were searched but there was no trace.

Emrys, a bachelor, was a former chairman of Colwyn Bay magistrates. He belonged to a tragic family ravaged on its female side by one of the cruellest illnesses in the world – Huntington's Chorea. My mother taught him in her Sunday school class and he came to her funeral. Emrys once worked in Australia. Where did he go?

Did he hurl himself off the cliffs? Or is he somewhere leading a new life? And why?

30

Thursday's man

It was an exclusive story in the *Sunday Express*. A rector in a sex scandal. Vicars and sex scandals have always been a big seller – but this one was different.

And in the ensuing Church in Wales disciplinary hearing, at which the rector was struck off, there came the quote that was the tabloid sub-editor's dream. 'Keep Thursday bonk-free for me,' he'd allegedly written in a note to a villager.

The claim that he'd been misbehaving broke in November 1996, and that Sunday morning I stood in the street outside his unpretentious church waiting to see if he turned up. He didn't. But when I gazed through the window I could see a familiar figure – Barry Morgan, the Bishop of Bangor. Like a shot, a *Daily Post* reporter and myself joined the congregation, occupying a pew near the back.

As surreptitiously as we could we slipped notebooks out of our pockets to take down what the bishop said. 'We pray for this parish and everyone in it who is feeling hurt this morning,' he said. That was enough.

Outside, Bishop Morgan, later Archbishop of Wales, announced: 'Serious allegations have been made about the rector. These are being investigated. In the meantime the rural dean will assume responsibility for the parish.'

Then the bishop spent an hour at the home of the rector who apparently claimed 'a conspiracy' against him. A church court later defrocked him. Even then there were some local housewives who claimed that he'd been highly popular and had 'galvanised the parish'.

But the court was damning, claiming that there would be 'a real element of danger' were he to remain in holy orders.

Many years on, I've saved his embarrassment by not naming him. But at the time he was the most discussed clergyman in Britain. Now he's back in the pulpit – but not in the Church in Wales.

31

Prayers for a hospice

BARBARA BUSH, MARGARET Thatcher, Edward Heath and Julian Lloyd Webber were among 60 personalities worldwide who provided a favourite prayer in aid of a hospice appeal.

A pensioner from Penrhyn Bay wrote more than 70 letters inviting people to provide a prayer. She then published a book, with all the cash going to the St David's Hospice Appeal in Llandudno.

Comedian Ken Dodd, president of the appeal, provided a Collect from the Book of Common Prayer.

Barbara Bush contributed what was described as an updated version of a 17th-century Nun's Prayer. It begins: 'Lord, Thou knowest better than I know myself that I am growing older and will someday be old. Keep me from the fatal habit of thinking I must say something on every subject and on every occasion. Release me from craving to straighten out everybody's affairs. Make me thoughtful but not moody; helpful but not bossy. With my vast store of wisdom it seems a pity not to use it all, but Thou knowest, Lord, that I want a few friends at the end.

'Keep my mind free from the recital of endless details; give me wings to get to the point. Seal my lips on my aches and pains...'

One of the most moving came from Simon Weston, the Welsh Guards' hero terribly burned during the attack on the *Sir Galahad* during the Falklands War. He chose 'The Welsh Guards' Collect' and wrote: 'The only place where I really feel secure and at peace is the Guards' Chapel, London – it's something I felt long before I was injured. I feel at peace with my companions left behind in the Falklands.'

Mrs Thatcher contributed her oft-quoted Prayer of St Francis of Assisi: 'Lord make me an instrument of Your peace.'

The most unusual came from the effervescent Edwina Currie MP, a prayer she once heard as Grace at a Showmen's Guild lunch:

'Oh Lord,

'Grant that we not be like porridge – heavy and slow to stir,

'Grant that we be like cornflakes – full of sunshine and quick to serve.'

The choice of Labour leader Neil Kinnock was from Ecclesiastes 3: 'To every thing there is a season, and a time to every purpose under the heaven: A time to be born and a time to die...'

Julian Lloyd Webber chose the 23rd Psalm.

Sir Wyn Roberts quoted Sir Thomas More's prayer:

'Lord, give me patience in tribulations and grace in everything to conform my will to Thine: that I may truly say: "Thy will be done on earth as it is in heaven..."'

Not surprisingly, the book sold like hot cakes. What a brilliant money-raising idea.

32

The day the sea invaded Towyn

I WILL ALWAYS remember the day in 1990 when the Towyn flood disaster happened. For our family it was a traumatic time, because we had just lost our three-year-old granddaughter Charlotte at Alder Hey Hospital.

What happened in Towyn was, with retrospect, entirely predicable. It only required a breach in the sea wall for the water to pour in and engulf 2,800 homes. Disastrous though it was, the miracle was that not a single life was lost, though a local doctor estimated that 50 may have died prematurely because of the trauma.

The flood led to 5,600 people fleeing their homes, the biggest peacetime evacuation in Britain. Some were accommodated at Bodelwyddan Castle, where families slept on the floor – dogs and all, and were visited by Prince Charles and Princess Diana.

According to a survey by the Welsh Consumer Council, the lack of insurance cover and the attitude of loss adjustors were the two most shocking findings. And, of course, the activities of cowboy builders. Of the homes flooded, 15 per cent were estimated to be without buildings insurance, and 40 per cent had not insured the contents.

Funds were set up to help victims who were under-insured or had none at all, which some said was unfortunate for those wise families who had in fact paid their premiums to protect their homes.

Two years later some were still living in caravans while their homes were repaired or insurance claims settled. The stink after the water had receded from flooded homes was appalling. Water poured a mile inland in parts of Towyn and Kinmel Bay, leaving a trail of misery.

Ronald Roberts, 65, was winched by helicopter from the roof of a van. Mrs Elsie Mortimer, 90, was trapped inside her home for four hours before rescue. Others were saved by RAF helicopters from rooftops and the roofs of garden sheds. Some awaited rescue up to their waists in filthy water in their own kitchens and dining rooms.

The stoicism of the inhabitants and the bravery of the rescue services shone like a beacon. And at least one romance blossomed from the heartbreak – Mary Poole and Bill Douglas, both 79, married after a whirlwind courtship in a residential home where they lived temporarily after their own houses were devastated.

Many insurance companies behaved shamefully towards the victims, with delay and procrastination upsetting hundreds of families who had suffered enough. Three years later Llandudno also suffered bad flooding, with hundreds of homes damaged and an enduring picture of a PC directing traffic when up to his waist in water.

No one involved during the Towyn floods will ever forget the misery which ensued after the fiercest sea in a century punched a hole through the wall which protected the main north Wales railway line. Later, a committee of MPs held a meeting in Towyn and I had to report it live for the BBC. Yet hundreds of houses have been built since on that flood plain. Will they never learn?

33

Don't always believe them

I DESPAIR THAT so much local journalism is being destroyed by the men in suits.

It is because of them that investigative journalism at a local level has all but disappeared. Instead, Press releases and official 'statements' are accepted without question.

Yet organisations, governments and councils will lie if it suits them. It should be the duty of journalists to expose them. They will try to restrict information if it suits them.

This did happen some years ago when there were frightening happenings at Wylfa Nuclear Power Station on Anglesey. I covered court hearings when shocking facts were revealed.

Nuclear Electric was ordered to pay £54,000 in fines and costs because of gases which had been released, luckily being blown out to sea. Later they picked up a bill of £388,000 at the crown court for health and safety breaches. They'd exceeded the permitted weekly amount of radioactive sulphur being discharged into the atmosphere. It was said that it was more by luck than judgement that there hadn't been a significant impact on the environment, though what that would have entailed wasn't explained. The Pollution Inspectorate said that, had a falling grab arm damaged fuel elements, there could have been a fire, and other gases such as iodine could have been released. This could have led to the evacuation of staff and the surrounding area. A fire in one of the fuelling channels would have produced a Scale 4 event, compared with Chernobyl's Scale 7.

'There have been no comparable incidents in the British nuclear fuel industry,' said the prosecution. There was a nine-hour delay before a decision was made to shut off a reactor, after discussions with the National Grid.

'THE CROWN WILL SAY THAT DELAY WAS INFLUENCED BY ECONOMIC REASONS BECAUSE THERE'S A PENALTY CLAUSE WHICH OPERATES IF THE REACTORS ARE SHUT OFF WITHOUT WARNING TO THE NATIONAL GRID.' What a devastating claim. I wonder if such penalty clauses still exist, putting cash before safety?

The defence case was simply that, in the event, no harm was done, the public was not at risk, and experienced experts had acted properly.

It was four days before news of the incident leaked out (pardon the pun!) and even during the case a Nuclear Electric official described it as 'a little beyond being minor'.

And this was the impertinent 'note to editors': 'In short, this is a technical prosecution for a technical breach of authorisation – it was never a major incident, it had no environmental implications, and it was fully reported locally and regionally at the time.

'It's certainly true that it's the first time HM Inspectorate of Pollution has prosecuted Nuclear Electric – or indeed any commercial electricity generator, we understand from HMIP's Press Office. IF THERE'S ANY REAL NEW LINE, THAT'S PROBABLY IT.'

That's a classic example of how major organisations try to manipulate the media, cheekily suggesting the angle that would be least damaging.

The tragedy is that because so many local and regional newspapers no longer 'do journalism', it's a lot easier for them to get away with it in the 21st century. Newspapers have neither the manpower nor the will to challenge and pose the important questions. And most of their resources are employed in finding 'clickbait'.

Nowadays police forces, councils and other official organisations either say nothing or send jargon-filled publicity handouts to understaffed local and regional newspapers which are often used in their entirety and without question, merely to fill space. No questions are asked about the authenticity of the claims being made. In my day we called them 'puffs' and treated them with caution. But too often that is no longer the case.

3 4

What an uplifting story

OF ALL THE thousands of stories in which I've been involved, one of the happiest and uplifting was in 1984. A tale which I told in newspapers and in a radio interview.

It was when a copy of a secret diary which Noel Good kept in Japanese prisoner of war camps arrived at the home of his 40-year-old daughter Mrs Mary Kiehn in Colwyn Bay. An American serviceman found it on a beach but, before handing it over to US intelligence, he made a copy of all the pages.

Then he eventually tracked down Mr Good's only daughter after enquiries at a village near Nottingham where he once played the organ. Mrs Kiehn told me: 'A vicar from Leicestershire rang me and asked if I was Noel Good's daughter. He said my father's diary had been found on a beach in Japan. I was amazed and in tears.'

A few days later a copy of the diary arrived by post – 100 pages which the American, Mel Blanton, had copied laboriously on a typewriter. His local paper in Illinois had serialised the diaries and offered to trace the family.

Mr Good, a gunner in the Royal Artillery, had escaped to Sumatra before the fall of Singapore with other members of his regiment. Then they had set sail again but their ship was sunk by Japanese bombers and he was captured and was a POW between 1942 and 1945.

First he was at a camp in Java, then later in Japan where he saw the atomic bomb attack on Nagasaki.

'The diary is really in the form of letters to my mum,

Margaret, and in places very sad. But it is wonderfully moving and I can almost hear my father speaking those words. The diary has convinced me more than ever that two things pulled him through – his love for my mother and his faith in God.'

Part of his diary, written in Java in 1942, said: 'This is your 31st birthday today sweetheart. How I wish I were with you. But we have a terrible lot to be thankful for. Looking back, all the troops who were sent to the Far East, except for the few who escaped to Australia, are either dead or taken prisoners.

'Therefore, although it is hard for both of us, I here as prisoner and you at home with no news of me, we are actually very fortunate. My worst trouble is the fear of your health being affected by the thought that I am dead.'

Mrs Kiehn said: 'Running through the letters is that my father knew he had many lucky escapes and felt that he was destined to get back to my mother. Once he even referred to me, although I wasn't even born, and said how he would like his daughter to be brought up when they had a family.'

She had her own theory about how the diary came to be washed ashore. 'The war was over but my father was very ill when the prisoners were released. I remember him telling me as a little girl that he was very envious as others left for home. Maybe he felt at that stage he would never get home to my mother and gave the diary to someone to bring back to her. But, as the ship left harbour, it hit a mine and everyone was lost. Perhaps that is how it came to be on the beach.'

Mr Good died in 1984 aged 73 – just 13 weeks after his wife Margaret's death. His daughter said: 'It was almost as if he had come to the end of his life because my mum had died. His story has a happy ending because he came back and he and my mother were inseparable. I'm sure he would have kept diaries for the other years he was in captivity. I wonder if they will ever be found?'

Another story from the Second World War was that of Ukrainian Peter Doroshenko who in 1995 learned, after half a century, that his parents were still alive. In June 1942 he had to say farewell to his mother and father when he was driven away in a horse and cart on the first part of a journey to Berlin to become a slave labourer. When he failed to return after the war, his name was carved on the village war memorial. In 1947 he'd come to Britain as a displaced person after being freed in Austria, then married Welsh-speaking Elizabeth, worked in the Conwy Valley as a gardener-handyman, and had a family of four children and ten grandchildren.

He'd not written to his parents, fearing a letter from the West might upset the Russians. When a party of managers from the Ukraine visited the University College of North Wales, Bangor, in 1995, one of them, from near Kiev, met Peter Doroshenko – and when he went home discovered that Peter's parents were still alive. He also learned that his father, the village postman, had been told by the Nazis that Peter had been hanged.

35

The greatest comedian ever

A FEW YEARS ago I saw him at a Press Club celebration in Liverpool, ad-libbing for 40 minutes in one of the most brilliant comedy feats I've ever witnessed.

I'd first set eyes on Ken Dodd when I was a cub reporter in Colwyn Bay. He would turn up at summer variety performances on the pier.

I heard him at the Arcadia, Llandudno, in 1988 on the day it was announced that tax fraud charges were being brought against him. It must rank as one of the most amazing performances of his career, because he cracked jokes until midnight despite what was hanging over him.

Fittingly, it was at the same theatre in August 1989 that he made his comeback after being cleared of fiddling the taxman. He got a standing ovation from eleven hundred – before his act had even begun. Afterwards, inevitably in the early hours, I interviewed him for Radio Wales.

Asked how it felt to be back at work, Ken replied: 'Delighted, plumptious.' Souvenir programmes were sold in aid of the local hospice for what was billed as the 'Celebration Laughter Show'.

They say that Ken Dodd had the biggest compendium of jokes in creation. I think he was the greatest comedian in the world.

His accountant who lived in Colwyn Bay said after the trial, generously: 'I'm pleased Ken has been cleared. It would have been terrible for him to go to prison. If what has been said to my detriment has helped him, then I swallow the pill.'

At a Llandudno Christmas show Ken quipped that he'd had a festive card from the Inland Revenue. 'It said, "'tis better to give than to receive".' A few weeks after his appearance at the 2017 Press Club Christmas lunch, he died. In heaven they must be laughing...

36

'The road to opportunity'

IN OCTOBER 1991 the tunnel beneath the River Conwy, constructed from giant immersed tubes which had been made at the same spot where the D-Day Mulberry harbours had been constructed, was opened by the Queen. There was the biggest security operation since the Investiture, with both the IRA and Meibion Glyndŵr felt capable of disrupting the event.

The then Sir Wyn Roberts, Minister for Wales, declared that it was the modern equivalent of the accomplishments of Telford who built the magnificent suspension bridge there in 1826, and Robert Stephenson's tubular rail bridge of 1849.

For many years Conwy, one of the finest medieval walled towns in Europe and a World Heritage Site, had been plagued by traffic jams – but the tunnel was to end them for ever. Mind you, there have been plenty of hold-ups with tunnel 'essential maintenance'.

The tunnel cost £190 million and was a vital part of a 60-mile dual carriageway between Chester and Bangor, costing more than £600 million – cheap by today's standards. Soon another 20-mile stretch was to be added to Holyhead, the road becoming part of a designated Euro-route.

Welsh Secretary Nicholas Edwards had chosen a tunnel despite its cost being considerably greater than had a high-level bridge been built across the estuary. He agreed that a bridge would have an unacceptable impact on the 13th-century castle and walls.

The tunnel bill was at that time the biggest single trunk

road contract ever awarded in Britain. A huge casting basin was built on the west side of the estuary in which six giant tubes, each the size of an aircraft carrier, were constructed. They were towed into the river, sunk into a trench which had been gouged out of the sand and mud, then plugged and sealed together to form the tunnel, just over half a mile long. Each of the sections weighed 30,000 tonnes and a waterproofing system guaranteed durability for at least 120 years. So there's another century to go! A month before the opening more than 20,000 people took part in a charity walk through the tunnel organised by Rotary. Some walkers had travelled miles for the occasion, others such as Wyn Roberts just a few from his home in the Conwy Valley. 'It was an historic, exciting day,' he enthused. Conwy's enduring beauty has ensured that, despite a bypass, its attraction will always remain. Not many towns are so lucky when by-passed – such as my home town of Colwyn Bay, split from its seafront by a railway and a dual carriageway.

Now the A55, due to a huge increase in traffic, has often been a nightmare due to accidents and unending roadworks. Environmentalists would doubtless be outraged, but maybe another dual carriageway should be built inland, taking a route over the mountains like the Romans did!

37

Political correctness

I MUST RETURN to this topic. I'm proud to say I've written many stories debunking the political correctness which stains our everyday life. As I've mentioned before, it's a question of journalistic honour that I have never used the word chair instead of chairman or chairwoman. Sometimes, to my displeasure, sub-editors have written it into my stories.

This nonsense all began about 25 years ago, remarkably a few years before the Blair government.

I got a hilarious if perhaps worrying insight into political correctness when covering the annual conference of the National Association of Probation Officers. Believe it or not, speakers were monitored for six 'isms' – racism (of course), sexism, disablism (a new word for me), heterosexism (sometimes a dirty word in today's culture), ageism and sizeism.

At the end of the conference a report was presented by 'monitors' which stated, with considerable understatement: 'Language is still a difficulty.'

The leader of the monitoring group pronounced, straight-faced: '"Paymaster" and "turning a blind eye" indicates that we need to remain vigilant.'

He explained afterwards: '"Paymaster" is sexist and makes an assumption that the male gender is the normal.'

The Association's chairwoman (to be strictly accurate she was described, but not by me, as 'chair') thanked the monitors for their work. 'It's a stressful and sometimes a thankless task,' she declared. What, stressful? Of all the definitions of stress I have ever heard that must be the least convincing. That's what I call murdering the meaning of words, like a courts' chief once saying it would be 'a tragedy' if north Wales didn't get its own jail.

A lesson that I'm sure isn't taught by the diversity moguls is that there are too many people for whom 'victimhood' has become a way of life, like the woman academic outraged in a lift by an innocent crack about the floor for 'ladies' lingerie'. Today, in every walk of life, there are victims-in-waiting prepared to be offended by the most innocuous of remarks. And an industry ready to pursue any perceived slight.

Councils are unsurpassed in their adherence to political correctness. A planning brief to Conwy Council described warm sunshine as 'passive solar gain'. An official explained: '"Passive solar gain" is a technical term which means not just to get sunshine but the heat you get from the sun.' As the Plain English Campaign put it: 'It's remarkable how councils have a knack of saying simple things in the most complicated way.'

There was the case of my old friend the late John Roberts MBE, winner of six bravery awards for some amazing rescues he carried out as head warden of Snowdonia National Park. He won an Employment Tribunal claim that he was unfairly sacked after failing to get a new post as newly designated 'warden and access manager'.

Among the reasons why a committee of six turned down 56-year-old John, it was claimed, was because he wouldn't embrace change, including the culture of 'Local Agenda 21 and Bio-Diversity after the Rio Summit'. But winning the action was a Pyrrhic victory because he wasn't entitled to any compensation. The tribunal ruled that there had been 'a lamentable lack of proper consultation'.

So incensed were former colleagues that they started a fund to meet his £4,000 in legal costs, and arranged a testimonial dinner. At least John got an enhanced pension for his 32 years' service.

'Local Agenda 21 and Bio-Diversity after the Rio Summit!' What planet do some of our administrators inhabit? Who puts them there? And how dare they insult a brave and faithful servant? The Authority later debated what the tribunal had said about them. But of course this was behind closed doors. I was proud to have broken the story of this scandal.

38

Lost in care

LOST IN CARE was the title of the report of Britain's longest ever and most searching inquiry into why official child care was apparently a misnomer in north Wales in a quarter of a century period.

For 203 days Sir Ronald Waterhouse, a retired high court judge, presided at a judicial inquiry costing £10 million in the well-appointed council offices in Ewloe, Flintshire, listening to stories of brutality, neglect and horror.

His brief was to look at what went wrong in children's homes in north Wales from 1974 into the 1990s. There were 250 live witnesses, others giving evidence in written statements, with testimony from social services chiefs in the former counties of Gwynedd and Clwyd, staff, councillors, police and senior Welsh Office officials.

There were sordid tales of cruelty and often homosexual sex, particularly at Bryn Estyn, near Wrexham, whose deputy head Peter Howarth was serving a ten-year sentence when he died before he could give evidence to the inquiry. Some evil and devious paedophiles, who had been undetected for years when holding high positions at children's homes or who were foster fathers, were also behind bars.

Gerard Elias QC, senior counsel to the tribunal, surprised many – including some lawyers – by his highly critical and hard-hitting opening. QC Anna Pauffley – now Dame Anna and later a Family Division judge – was rebuked by Sir Ronald when she suggested that the tribunal had been unfair to some of the

106 social workers and managers she represented. Sir Ronald described her comments as offensive and took exception to her claim that 'very little effort has been made by the tribunal to achieve fairness'. She protested about the 'hounding' in cross-examination of a couple accused of a catalogue of torture and depravity when fostering two sisters in the late 1970s. It became obvious, she said, that it was 'a spectacular fabrication – the product of a disturbed and troubled mind'.

From the start it appeared to me that often there was a presumption of guilt.

I've read *The Secret of Bryn Estyn: The Making of a Modern Witch Hunt* in which the author Richard Webster forensically dissected what was said at the tribunal and the assumptions made. He didn't deny that abuse took place, but challenged the extent that was alleged and that it was the norm in residential care. And he attacked the highly dangerous stratagem of police trawling for 'evidence' from suggestible people raised in care, including those in prison or living in a deprived subculture in which the lure of compensation, whatever the truth, would be attractive.

Some teachers and social workers, completely innocent, had been roused from their beds in front of their own families in dawn raids on their homes and taken to police stations for questioning. I know of one official so worried about being condemned that he died prematurely. A senior detective was criticised, wrongly in my opinion, for following his instinct for truth as he had done successfully throughout his career.

I was told about a clergyman who was wrongly accused when, in fact, he was in a different town at the time. And another former social worker who was told sarcastically at the tribunal that he had a selective memory. It was only later he realised the reason that he couldn't recognise the names of girls who had been in his care when read to him was because it was their married names that were quoted.

Yes, and I'm convinced that many children WERE abused and were treated with unkindness that should not be tolerated in a civilised country. Some of those who gave evidence, of both sexes, had made a success of their lives despite suffering abuse and indignity in their childhood. Clearly some of those in charge were paedophiles. But, equally as clearly, there were carers who were decent and conscientious.

Such was the atmosphere which seemed to prevail of there being no smoke without fire that it was difficult, even for reporters who spent most of their lives in court, to gauge the truth. Even the names of two prominent Tories were mentioned as possible abusers which prompted Sir Ronald to observe that it was embarking in the realm of fantasy, and that it showed the nature of some of the allegations.

One young man claimed he'd been driven to Merseyside and subjected to male rape. The 'aggressor' had to wait weeks before he could answer the allegation – by producing a note from a surgeon testifying that, because of an injury, he had a prosthetic organ! There were claims, proved to be entirely false, of a Masonic conspiracy, and of senior police officers being shielded by their colleagues.

Alleged abused and alleged abusers each had their own supporters, their own agendas, each convinced of their case. It provided an unsavoury background.

After the Waterhouse Report was published there was a furious reaction from the Bryn Estyn Staff Support Group, which claimed it had 'made a mockery of the British judiciary's reputation for fair play'. Acknowledging that abuse had occurred, it added: 'It is the Group's belief that the true tragedy of North Wales is the tragedy of false allegations of sexual abuse which have been made on an unprecedented scale.'

At the end of their ten-year probe into abuse, North Wales Police said they were pleased to have been vindicated and cleared of 'unfounded attacks on our integrity'. Det. Chief Supt. Peter Ackerley, who led the inquiry, said many officers had been upset by 'fanciful, untruthful and unsupported allegations'.

Rowan Williams, the Archbishop of Wales – later Archbishop of Canterbury – preached at a service in St Asaph Cathedral 'to reaffirm the value of the child' after the Waterhouse Report. He said they were mourning the fact that a network of agencies and individuals had failed to create a trustworthy environment, inflicting wounds on several generations.

One prayer was for those angry at being violated and abused, and also for those falsely accused. With recent revelations about appalling abuse perpetrated through the years by Roman Catholic priests, the Archbishop mentioned, perhaps with some prescience, that the Church's record in the care of children 'gives it no right to take the moral high ground'.

What has never been disclosed is how many millions of pounds were paid in compensation to victims of abuse. The government vowed to take action to prevent any more care home scandals. Yet, while Sir Ronald and his two colleagues were still compiling their report, MPs voted to lower the age for gay sex to 16. This was despite Sir Ronald having observed that the age of consent for homosexual sex 'was of some importance to the fate of children in care'.

MPs were conspicuous by their absence from hearings of the tribunal. They didn't hear the sordid evidence about vulnerable youths in care who were victims of depravity.

Yet they voted for 16 year olds to be old enough for homosexual sex. Too young, of course, to drive or drink – or fight for their country. 'Liberalising the gay sex law' is how MPs described what they'd done. At least the then Archbishop of Canterbury, the redoubtable George Carey, raised a voice of protest to what anyone who was at the tribunal would be tempted to label a paedophile's charter. I wrote a feature in the *People* attacking what had happened.

With the help of son Glyn, I covered the tribunal from day one to the finish, having special commissions from HTV, the *Daily Post* and *Western Mail*. National papers gave prominence to the start and the eventual report, with very little in between. Once they heard that a peer of the realm was not involved in abuse, many of them lost interest.

Were the lessons learned? A few years later, in the minutes of Conwy Council, a problem was mentioned about getting sufficient members to form a rota to visit care homes – exactly one of the criticisms voiced at the tribunal. No lessons learned there, then.

In 2009 a 20-year-old man, John Garcia, who had lived on Anglesey most of his life was deported to the Philippines from Britain – to a land he could barely remember from the time he was four and whose language he didn't understand.

I'd written many stories about his battle to stay in Britain but he had few friends either in Parliament or the Welsh Assembly. For Garcia was an ASBO tearaway – not a terrorist, nor gangster – who had made a thorough nuisance of himself in his home village of Pentraeth. It was in a detention centre that it was realised that he'd never applied for UK citizenship, unlike his mum and other members of his family, though he'd attended school on Anglesey and could even speak Welsh. Immigration tribunals rejected his pleas and he was deported, leaving his mum in Britain.

What has this to do with the child abuse inquiry? Just that some of his crimes were committed while he was a juvenile, not an adult. So he couldn't be considered beyond redemption. John Garcia needed a champion but didn't have one – just like those victims of child abuse in the old days found to their distress. There was no one to listen or who was prepared to fight. After the tribunal this wasn't supposed to happen to young people. I know probation officers who consider that the deporting of John Garcia was an outrage. I agree and wish I could have done more.

In the youth court I've reported cases where homeless teenagers have been sent by social services to live in flats or at run-down hotels where drug addicts were also accommodated.

I've no doubt the Waterhouse Report has resulted in many administrative changes, with 'i's dotted and 't's crossed. And there's also the appointment of a Children's Commissioner for Wales.

But as to whether all vulnerable youngsters are now given the protection and care they deserve, I have my doubts.

39

Fake news?

IT WAS DONALD Trump, the biggest fake of all, who coined the expression in his bid to bully and ridicule the media.

In my long experience I've come across many stories that are exaggerated and elaborated and I suppose I am as guilty as the next journalist. But fakery – never!

I know of two examples, both apocryphal. In his excellent autobiography Michael Buerk refers to his time as a young evening paper reporter in south Wales and how a rival youngster, on a newspaper with a news editor wonderfully described as 'legendarily deranged' and as a megalomaniac with a volcanic temper, decided in desperation to invent a story about a pretty young girl and an animal. He chose the longest street in Newport as the address and all went well until next morning. Then pictures were demanded, TV teams arrived for a follow-up and there was no alternative but to confess. There was eventually a happy ending for the reporter because later he was to become a TV news editor.

The other item of fake news involved the two competing evening papers in Manchester. An *Evening News* reporter, tired of being stalked by his rival, entered a phone box, left the door ajar so that his voice could be heard outside and pretended to dictate a 'story' about a winged horse appearing at the Salford carnival. Apparently, the non-story duly appeared in the *Evening Chronicle*, and the *Evening News* reporter got a call from his news editor demanding a follow-up. I'm told that even when it was explained that the story was fake, he was ordered to produce 'something' about the only winged horse in the world!

So where does 'the dead-tree Press', to quote *Private Eye*, go from here? It was not until the early 1800s that newspapers became established, with coffee houses and pubs turned into reading rooms. But it was not until the late 1800s that the Press really became free, and popular papers were born. I can't believe that they will ever go completely out of fashion.

Technology means that today's news can be read on phones, laptops and iPads. Some newspaper groups are coming to terms with this, with their own news websites and news feeds, and even making a small profit from them.

But you can't, with any comfort, enjoy the weekend supplements on a mobile phone, nor read enthralling features, editorials – or even those fascinating holiday ads. And there's nothing more satisfying than relaxing with a good 'read of the paper'. Long may it continue. So let's be optimistic!

Epilogue

IN THE SUMMER of 2014 we stayed in Charleston, South Carolina, where sadly nine prominent black churchmen were gunned down in June 2015. We'd found Charleston one of the friendliest (and loveliest) places we'd ever visited. Despite the tragedy the gunman's intention to divide was thwarted, with families and church leaders 'forgiving' him. And President Obama, unforgettably, leading the singing of 'Amazing Grace'.

In New York we went to the 101st floor of a new tower to gaze at a magnificent view of the city. Also we visited the nearby St Paul's Church, a sanctuary and inspiration during the agony of the Twin Towers atrocity. Looking at the photographs and messages, even this lapsed Christian had to admit: this is an inspiring religion.

Now it is 2019. I've been blessed to reach 86 and life is still good. Shirley and I took a wonderful (and I tease my children, inheritance-busting!) 21-day voyage from Dubai to Southampton, once again on the magnificent *Queen Mary 2* last year.

We saw the glories of Petra in Jordan, the 'Red Rose City' carved into the rocks, possibly dating back to 300 BC. And Jordan took us back to the time of Moses with its Old Testament history, with Bedouin shepherds, some of them women, looking after sheep and goats. Also I saw the Suez Canal once again, after 64 years, this time in some luxury and no danger.

It was a never-to-be-forgotten holiday, only to be surpassed by the birth of our first great-grandchild, Florence Alexandra Bellis, to Luke (son of Nigel and Carol) and Heidi.

The year 2018 had its sadness, too. My sister Joan's funeral was on what would have been her 93rd birthday. I recalled in a eulogy how ex-pupils, some even grandparents now, would come to her in the street, smiling in happy recollection, and saying 'I remember you Mrs Sattler'. What a memory to leave behind.

Another great sadness was my quite accidental discovery that two of my great-uncles, brothers of my taid (grandfather), had died within a month of each other on the Somme in the summer of 1916. They have no known graves. How awful is war...

Also from Y Lolfa:

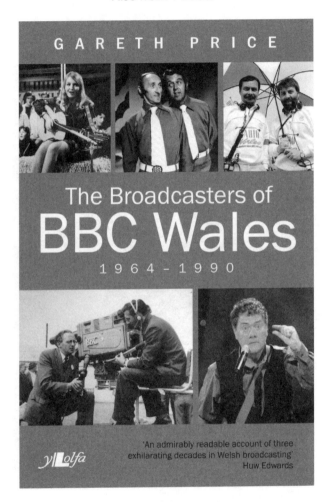

GARETH PRICE

The Broadcasters of
BBC Wales
1964 - 1990

'An admirably readable account of three
exhilarating decades in Welsh broadcasting'
Huw Edwards

y Lolfa

£12.99

Raising an Echo

Glyn
Mathias

Autobiography

£9.95

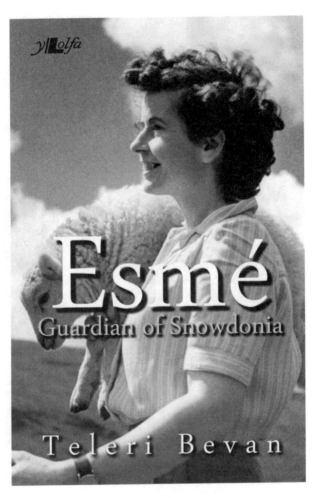

Esmé
Guardian of Snowdonia

Teleri Bevan

£9.95

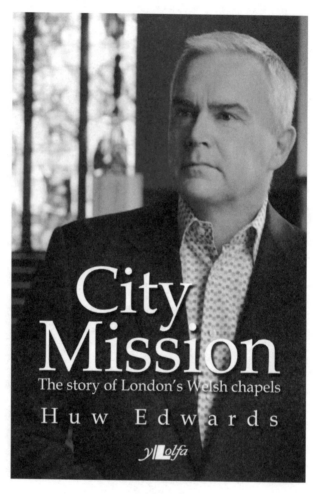

City
Mission
The story of London's Welsh chapels

H u w   E d w a r d s

yl Lolfa

£14.95 (pb)
£24.95 (hb)

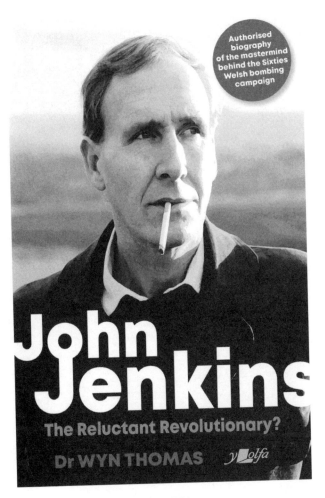

Authorised biography of the mastermind behind the Sixties Welsh bombing campaign

John Jenkins

The Reluctant Revolutionary?

Dr WYN THOMAS

y Lolfa

£19.99 (hb)